ET   5367   8

Crazy States

Crazy States

A Counterconventional Strategic Problem

Yehezkel Dror
The Hebrew University of Jerusalem
and The World Institute
Jerusalem

Heath Lexington Books
D.C. Heath and Company
Lexington, Massachusetts
Toronto   London

**To the Memory of my Father
Dr. Isidor Friemann**

Table of Contents

List of Tables xi

Introduction xiii

Chapter 1 Common Fallacies in American Strategic Studies 1

Fallacy 1–"Was" Equals "Is" Equals "Will Be" 4
Fallacy 2–"Should" Equals "May" Equals "Will" 5
Fallacy 3–Conflict is Stylized 7
Fallacy 4–Crisis Is Bad 8
Fallacy 5–The Adversary Is a Person 9
Fallacy 6–Adversaries Are Fixed 9
Fallacy 7–Strategic Policy Is Separate from
 Domestic Policies 9
Fallacy 8–Political Goals Are beyond
 Strategic Analysis 11
Fallacy 9–What Is Good for the United States Is
 Good for All Others . . . Up to a Certain Point 12
Fallacy 10–Everyone Wants What We Want 14
Fallacy 11–Development Will Help 15
Fallacy 12–Power Breeds Responsibility 16
Fallacy 13–Risk Is Minimized 17
Fallacy 14–Everyone Plays It Cool 17
Fallacy 15–Means Serve Ends 19
Fallacy 16–Negotiations Help 19
Fallacy 17–Agreements Are Kept 20
Fallacy 18–World Opinion Is Real/Unreal 20
Summary 21

Chapter 2 The Concept of Crazy States 23

Chapter 3 Probability of Crazy States 31

Scenario 1. United States Transformation
 into a Crazy State 33

Scenario 2. The Soviet Union Transforms
into a Crazy State 34

Chapter 4 **External-Action Capabilities of Crazy States** 41

Conventional Military External-Action Instruments 49
Nuclear Military External-Action Instruments 50
Infraconventional Military External-Action
Instruments 53
Ultraconventional Military External-Action
Instruments 54

Chapter 5 **Some Preferable Strategies for Crazy States** 59

Deception 63
Infiltration and Take-Over from Within 63
Conversion 64
Erosion 65
Isolation 65
Alliances 65
Provocation 66
Blackmail 67
Occupation 69
Destruction 69
Timing 70

Chapter 6 **Some Preferable Countercraziness Strategies** 73

Substrategy 1. Reduce Conditions Which Encourage
Crazy States, or Which Encourage Them to
Become Crazier 73
Substrategy 2. Reduce Conditions for Development
of External-Action Capabilities by Possible
Crazy States 74
Substrategy 3. Early Detecting of Emerging
Possible Crazy States 76
Substrategy 4. Activate Particular Controls to
Hinder Emerging Crazy States from Developing
a Significant External-Action Capability 77

Substrategy 5. Reverse Trend Toward Craziness   78
Substrategy 6. Avoid Encouraging Craziness by
   Rewarding It   78
Substrategy 7. Counterbalance Emerging Crazy States   79
Substrategy 8. Deter Crazy States   80
Substrategy 9. Actively and Intensely Pursue
   Reinforced Versions of Substrategies 4, 5, and 6   82
Substrategy 10. Prepare Local Multiactors for
   Countercraziness Action   82
Substrategy 11. Destroy External-Action Capability   84
Substrategy 12. Stimulate Revolt   84
Substrategy 13. Occupy Crazy State   84
Substrategy 14. Limit Damage That Can Be Caused By
   Crazy State   85
Substrategy 15. Bargain to Win Time   86
Substrategy 16. Capitulate   87

Chapter 7   **Expected Countercraziness Behavior**   93

Chapter 8   **Significance of the Crazy States Issue**   97

Selected Readings   103

Notes   107

About the Author   113

Index   115

List of Tables

Table

2-1	Dimensions of Craziness	27
2-2	Main Prototypes of Craziness	29
3-1	Some Hypothetical Transformations of Present States into Crazy States	35
4-1	Simplified Model of Variables that Shape External-Action Capability	43
4-2	Maximum External-Action Capability of Different States	55
4-3	Levels of External-Action Capabilities of Crazy States	56
4-4	Main Prototypes of Possible Crazy States	57
5-1	External-Action Instruments and Preferable Substrategy Components	62
5-2	Some Preferable Strategies for Possible Crazy States	71
6-1	Mutual Images of Pax Americana-Sovietica	88

Introduction

This book is devoted to a neglected subject, and, for just that reason, an all important one: Crazy states. The main subject is crazy behavior in its security and international perspectives.

It is, indeed, a source of surprise and amazement that the possibilities of crazy states are nearly completely neglected in contemporary strategic thinking.[1] Admittedly, the probability of crazy states is not very high; but history is not made by highly probable behavior; rather, unusual and exceptional phenomena play critical roles in the shaping of human history. Therefore, though the credibility of my images of crazy states may seem to some observers to be quite low, the relevance of crazy states if and when they occur is so high as to deserve significant attention, preparation, prevention, and treatment. The skeptic needs only to consider Nazi Germany, which can serve as a striking and radical demonstration of the possibility of crazy states and their implications for the international order and the security of various countries. Recent occurrences also should bring home the possibility of crazy states in the form of noncountry groups.

The occurrence of crazy behavior is not easy to predict. But—as will be explained in this book—the probability of crazy states is increasing; more and more cases, both on the country and the noncountry level, should be expected. Also, thanks to the advancement of modern technology, the capabilities of crazy states and their potential impact are increasing on a very steep curve. Therefore, far from being a purely intellectual exercise, the subject deserves intense attention and careful preparations.

The main purposes of this book are to contribute to strategic analysis, discourse, and action by calling attention to this neglected, and highly important, possibility. Though this book is written on a high level of abstraction, a number of proposals are included from time to time to illustrate concepts and to suggest the applied significance of the analysis. At the same time, I hope that the abstract theory will be a very practical tool in facing the danger of crazy states.

The methodological foundations of this book are policy sciences on one hand and strategic analysis on the other hand. Combining the approaches of policy analysis with the concrete subject matter of strategic studies, I try to approach the issue within a global systems framework; but, in distinction to other uses of a general systems framework in the study of international relations, I try to adopt a policy orientation designed to tie in the analysis with the needs and characteristics of preferable policy-making.

In distinction from traditional scientific endeavors, this study is not directed at the discovery of regularities and rules which describe and explain reality. Policy analysis—as policy sciences as a whole—is directed towards the improvement of policy-making with the help of systematic knowledge, structured rationality and organized creativity.[2] The appropriate criterion for evaluating this study, as all other policy analyses, is not the extent of contribution to scientific knowledge in the traditional sense, but the contributions of the study to the understanding of policy issues and to improved policy-making.

The main tools of my analysis are prototypes of crazy countries, the meaning and significance of which is examined on a generalized level, with main attention to the more extreme and "pure" types.[3] However abstract, I regard this approach as appropriate for a first cut at a difficult and neglected issue. But I realize that my treatment is preliminary and tentative, requiring much more detailed and penetrating continuation. Indeed, in view of the lack of attention to possible crazy international phenomena in international relations theory and in actual policies alike, one main purpose of my study is to sensitize both scholars and policy-makers to this issue and to encourage more theoretic and applied attention to it.

The book deals with the future. Therefore, and because I regard the past as an unreliable guide for future policies, I avoid historic cases other than short mentions for purposes of illustration. I avoid current acute problems, so as not to mix up the general message of this book with passing crises. But the interested reader will have little difficulty in applying parts of my concepts to a number of present issues faced by the international system as a whole, and by various countries—including the United States—in particular.

More important than formal methodologies for explaining the genesis of this book may be the author's personal history. Coming from Israel, a small country surrounded by adversaries, I am more sensitive to the possibilities and implications of seemingly irrational political behavior than either American strategists or the American public in general. The dangers facing my own country and my personal background carry with them biases of their own. But, after all, biases are unavoidable, and progress in trying to overcome them depends significantly on contrasting the implications of different biases, so as to gain a better overall perspective. At least, this book should provide an additional perspective on strategic problems and it may shed somewhat different light on issues and problems.

This book is designed to penetrate into the issues of crazy states by moving back and forth between different points of view and by examining the same issues from the perspective of different multiactors.[a] To provide a broad

---

[a]To avoid the fallacy of comparing countries to individuals, I am using the term, multiactors. A multiactor is a unit composed of more than a single individual, for example, a group, an organization, a country. Similarly, one should speak about a multiadversary, rather than about an adversary. But to keep neologisms limited, I will use the term adversary, after having warned the reader to beware of unintended connotations.

perspective, the first chapter discusses some common fallacies in United States strategic studies which constitute blind spots and prevent correct perception of craziness as an important phenomenon. This chapter also brings out the significance of extreme cases for testing the validity of strategic assumptions and explicating the limits of their domain of validity. The second and third chapters are devoted to the presentation of the concept of crazy states—the third tries to make a case for the probability of crazy states. The case for crazy states as a main problem for the international system and for security strategy is stated in Chapter 4, which deals with external action capabilities. The main finding is that even minor crazy countries, and perhaps, even crazy noncountry units, can achieve troublesome capabilities on the nuclear, infraconventional, and ultraconventional levels. Through a cross-tabulation of different kinds of crazy states with various levels of capabilities, we conclude with a set of possible crazy states (PCS).

In Chapter 5, we move to the point-of-view of possible crazy states. Here, a series of preferable strategies designed to maximize achievements of PCS are developed. Then, some variables shaping real strategies are considered, so as to estimate the probabilities of any one of the preferable strategies occurring.

Countercraziness strategies constitute the main subject matter for Chapters 6 and 7. Chapter 6 deals with preferable countercraziness strategies, including countercraziness actions ranging from recognition of the possibilities of crazy behavior, its prevention, detection, and reversal; to decapacitation, containment, destruction; and, under some circumstances, capitulation. The chapter reflects the perspective of different multiactors and concludes with some implication for accepted doctrines, such as intervention and deterrence.

In Chapter 7, we move from preferable behavior to expected behavior. Introducing into our analysis features of real-life policy-making, we make an effort to predict some probable reactions to PCS. Real expected countercraziness strategies are evaluated and are found quite inadequate to face PCS.

Chapter 8 concludes the book. On the basis of examination, I arrive at the conclusion that PCS are a main danger—to the world, to the United States, and to each country. Therefore, the problem of PCS must be regarded as a very salient one. Even if PCS are viewed as pure type constructs more than as really possible phenomena, there is sufficient probability for some approximation in reality to warrant preparation of counterstrategies and their activation.

In light of the nature of this book as a preliminary policy analysis, I avoid the usual apparatus of scholastic studies. Footnotes and references are kept to a minimum. Instead, the interested reader is referred to some of the relevant literature in the Selected Readings at the end of the book.

I am grateful to my colleagues for highly appreciated help and advice, and in particular, I am much indebted to Fred Ikle, Edward Quade and some anonymous reviewers for their important comments. I also appreciate the valuable help provided by some of my graduate students and present or former assistants at the Hebrew University of Jerusalem, and in particular, to Avigdor Haselkorn, Michael Hendel, Michael Horn and Jeffrey Stutz. The special nature of this book makes it all the more necessary to emphasize that I alone am responsible for the ideas presented in it.

Yehezkel Dror

Crazy States

1 Common Fallacies in American Strategic Studies

Underlying all analysis and all purposeful activities are tacit theories, including perceptions, understandings, assumptions, and concepts of reality (including the past, the present, and the future). It is tacit theories which provide a basic mechanism for higher mental processes. Implicitly, we try out different ideas and alternatives, and adopt those which, according to our individual and highly personal tacit theories, meet our criteria. Science presumes to explicate its tacit theories, to subject them to the stubborn facts of reality, and to clearly identify their degree of similarity or identity with the real world. But, even science cannot overcome the fundamental dependence of the human mind on tacit theories, at least on the level of metatheories. Nonscientific activities are all the more dependent on tacit theories, the validity of which are very seldom subjected to testing. The naive hope that we modify or even abandon some of our tacit theories automatically with the help of experience is clearly wrong. Phenomena such as the reduction of postdecisional dissonance (i.e., to perceive goals to fit results) and the long time-span between action and results inhibit much learning from experience and permit tacit theories to be unchanged, never mind their low degrees of validity and similarity with reality.

Not only are tacit theories unavoidable for psychological, cultural, and linguistic reasons, but they also fulfill positive functions. They provide the principles by which we order the infinite facts of reality and they permit us to identify relevant variables and to interrelate them into meaningful entities (systems). But the very usefulness of tacit theories increases the dangers of incorrect ones. By controlling the selection of facts and their processing, every tacit theory tends to reinforce itself, explaining away all contradictory evidence that cannot be ignored in terms that stem from the same premise.

Strategic studies and strategic planning are especially prone to incorrect tacit theories. Not being deeply rooted in the scientific tradition, strategic studies often fail to explicate their tacit theories, other than within the technical domain of systems analysis and its tools, such as sensitivity testing. The results of strategic studies, even when they have impact on real policies, are impossible to identify (and are often far off in the future) so that revision of the underlying tacit theories on the bases of feedback is very difficult. Furthermore, strategic studies deal with potential behavior of adversaries who are difficult to understand and who often deliberately try to camouflage their intentions and

1

capabilities. As a result, strategic studies tend to be very mistaken in their tacit theories. The more serious mistakes take the form of what I call fallacies.

In the United States, strategic studies are especially dependent on tacit theories and, therefore, exposed to dangerous fallacies. America deals with the whole world. Therefore, tacit theories to screen reality and process it into manageable images are all the more essential to her, though the chance that any one tacit theory will do justice to the heterogeneity of the world is very low, indeed. Division of Labor in the policy-making community is of insufficient help because (a) all members share a similar policy culture and, therefore, many elements reflect the same tacit theories; and (b) insofar as different components have different tacit theories, relative impact on policy is determined by relative power, which is not causally related to the validity of their tacit theories in respect to the issues being decided. A smaller country dealing with a limited number of international multiactors has a better opportunity to learn to know its specific environment and to establish more valid tacit theories—though this is not always the case. (Furthermore, such a country may run into serious problems when somehow a new adversary enters the scene, one who cannot be handled in terms of its earlier successful tacit theories.) But, for a universal multiactor to know its global environment—this requires a level of sophistication beyond present policy-relevant knowledge—and far beyond present characteristics of politics and policy-making in the United States and other universal multiactors. (The same is true, often even more so, in other countries; but, other countries may not need so high a sophistication in order to handle less complex issues.)

A first requirement to reduce and overcome fallacies in strategic studies is the advancement of scientific methodologies, preferably in conjunction with the development of policy science as a whole. An improved scientific methodology for strategic studies should include, as a main element, better modes of explication of tacit theories, as described in the following examples.[a]

[a]Improved and more explicit methodologies in strategic studies should also help to overcome some other widespread weaknesses, such as naive treatment of political goals and objectives which are above and beyond strategic studies; neglect of broad and long-range strategic considerations when deciding on military hardware (which unavoidably and severely constraints future strategic options); and the tendencies to focus narrowly on specific and detailed issues, to make artificial and unjustified assumptions on boundary conditions, and to neglect important exogenous variables.

It is interesting to inquire why strategic studies do not utilize improved methodologies. Among the reasons for this situation, the following seem to play a prominent role: organizational conservatism, especially strong in military organizations; resistance by the military to methods developed mainly by civilians; scarcity of suitable methods and of high-quality professionals able to use them (and, in the United States, the unwillingness of some such professionals to devote themselves to strategic issues); lack of agreement on the usefulness of these methods in respect to real strategic issues; hostilities between the foreign affairs community and the defense community, which inhibit work on in-between issues such as the broader political goals of strategic planning; and resistance to the shift in power involved in greater reliance on scientific methods of analyses and on the professionals who enjoy a near monopoly on the knowledge required for doing so.

1. Systematic monitoring of predictions and recommendations of strategic studies and comparison of predicted results and actual occurrences. Despite all difficulties, such comparisons may improve strategic studies by providing at least some qualitative feedback.[b]
2. Redundancy in strategic studies in order to get some diversity in the tacit theories—and thus some insurance against serious mistakes resulting from dependence on any one theory. Such redundancy should include many overlapping projects within any one country and multicultural approaches based on projects pursued both in and by different countries.[c]
3. Revised methods for explaining, describing, simulating, and predicting the behavior of other international multiactors, such as: (a) total simulation groups (which for an extended time imitate in all respects the life style and decision culture of another international multiactor); (b) utilization of persons affiliated with other cultures for explanation, simulation, and prediction; and (c) operational code elaboration and constant reformulation in respect to international multiactors.[d]
4. Testing of strategic studies by subjecting their hypotheses to hypothetical cases, including both historic and synthesized, and factual and counterfactual ones. Such test cases should bring underlying tacit theories out into the open and stimulate their conscious reconsideration.

The fallacies in United States strategic studies are closely related to the subject of this book for two main reasons.

1. Neglect of the crazy state problem is a main symptom of strategic studies fallacies in operation and demonstrates the hold of those fallacies over United States policy.
2. Studying the crazy state problem can help strategists revise some tacit theories and overcome some of their strategic fallacies. (This in itself would justify the serious consideration of crazy states.)

Therefore, some exploration of a few outstanding fallacies in United States strategic studies is an appropriate introduction to the main body of this book.

---

[b]Even in respect to military doctrines, such feedback is difficult to get, though technically, it should be an easy and natural result of good military staff work. The following quotation from a report by General O.P. Weyland on the Korean War is revealing.

An astonishing facet of the Korean War was the number of old lessons that had to be relearned. . . . It appears that these lessons either were forgotten or were never documented—or if documented, were never disseminated.[1]

[c]The tendency in United States strategic considerations to adopt a condescending attitude to strategic studies done in other countries, who naturally work from different tacit theories, is both a symptom and a contributing cause of fallacies in United States strategic studies. Especially striking are reactions to some French strategic studies.

[d]The idea of operational codes was put forth quite some time ago.[2]

The following list of fallacies is based on an impressionistic survey of published United States strategic studies.[e] Not all fallacies appear in any one study, but there are only a few studies which are free from most of the fallacies. Many strategic studies are outstanding and even brilliant—but this seems to increase susceptibility to fallacies, perhaps because elaboration of brilliant ideas draws attention away from underlying tacit theories. In an area such as strategic studies, one can always hope that classified material is superior to open literature and avoids the main fallacies. But this is usually an illusionary hope. In the United States, basic strategic thinking seems to penetrate quickly into open literature. Since the fallacies presented here deal with basic ideas and not with intelligence estimates, weapons performance, and contingency planning, there is little reason to assume that analogous classified materials are qualitatively much superior to them.

Many of the fallacies overlap, and for other purposes, a different listing may be preferable. But, for my purposes, the details are not so important. What we are interested in is the general *Gestalt* of fallacies in United States strategic studies,[f] especially as relevant to the problem of crazy states. Later, we will have many occasions to refer to these fallacies and to use them in the context of the crazy states problem. At present, we are interested in a concise examination of some of the main fallacies.

Fallacy 1—"Was" Equals "Is" Equals "Will Be"

Understanding the present in terms of the past and predicting the future in terms of the present and the past, constitutes a main fallacy of strategic studies.

Like many fallacies, this one is deeply rooted in basic patterns of the human mind, namely the hard-to-avoid reliance on past regularities to analyze and predict the future. Furthermore, this fallacy can in fact be validated if we take a statistical point of view. Most events that happened in the past were similar in many features to events which had happened in the earlier past. Nevertheless, history—as seen with presently available knowledge—is full of irregularities and even jumps—and in no sense constitutes a direct line of development in the time

---

[e]The interested reader who wants to check for himself the validity of my list of fallacies should start with the debate on the ABM, which is very dense in extreme manifestations of nearly all the fallacies. Official documents also reflect many of the fallacies.

[f]The United States has no monopoly on strategic fallacies. In fact, many of the fallacies discussed in this chapter are shared by strategic studies in the United States and in England, and some seem to be nearly universal. Other countries, such as France and the Soviet Union, have strategic fallacies of their own. A comparative study of such fallacies in different countries would be very revealing. But in this chapter, I limit myself to those fallacies which are very pronounced in United States strategic studies, without referring to their distribution in the strategic studies of other countries.[3]

dimension.[g] Therefore, a close look at history repudiates this fallacy that what will happen is similar to what is happening and to what happened earlier. And, it is this noncontinuity which constitutes some of the main strategic challenges. Therefore, when trying to deal with potentially catastrophic future possibilities, we must be able to envisage unprecedented seemingly remote occurrences which have not formed a strong imprint on our frame of reference. (At the same time, many strategic studies tend to the opposite fallacy, namely, the assumption that the near future will be very different from the present. Many peace studies are prone to this fallacy. Paradoxically, both fallacies sometimes appear in the same study—resulting in a view of a future of sudden changes, but changes based on the past.)

Well known and much condemned is the image of the military professional who prepares for the last war. This image, based on what happened in many general staffs after World War I, is in itself an illustration of the propensity to regard what is happening now and what will happen in the future on the basis of what happened in the past. Less recognized are the many expressions of this fallacy in strategic studies. There was a time when strategic analysts claimed to be much more geared to the future than were the professional military. The very term unconventional warfare symbolizes some tendencies in strategic studies to deal with the future in terms different from the past. But, by now, the idea of unconventional warfare has become, itself, quite conventional and strategic studies are, in many respects, prone to Fallacy 1. The tendency to perceive future strategic contingencies in terms of past happenings illustrates this fallacy in operation. Another Korea, another Vietnam, another Munich, another Berlin crisis—these are among the important implicit or explicit concepts used in strategic studies. Not less pronounced is the failure of most strategic literature (with some outstanding exceptions) to consider what I call counterconventional possibilities, such as crazy states—a failure caused in part by this fallacy.

I do not want to overstate the case. But, change is often regarded as incremental and, therefore, as something that can be handled by precepts based on the past; even rapid change is expected to follow lines regarded as normal in terms of the past. This is, in part, misleading, particularly in respect to strategic issues (which often become issues exactly because they are dissimilar to the perceived past and, therefore, were not predicted). Especially in time of rapid transformation of global society and nonincremental progress in science, the implications of this fallacy can be very serious.

Fallacy 2—"Should" Equals "May" Equals "Will"

The tendency to view future possibilities and future reality as approximating what we would like them to look like is another recognized and widespread

---

[g]This fallacy in strategic studies is closely related to widespread related fallacies in the study of history.[4]

(though not universal) human phenomenon. It is here that—as already mentioned—strategic studies tend sometimes to jump into an assumption exactly opposite to Fallacy 1, namely, that the near future will be very different from the present and near past.

An illustration of this fallacy is the inability of participants in strategic games to distinguish between behavior *expected* from the actor (or multiactor) they are simulating, and the behavior which they regard as *optimal* for their actor (or multiactor). In an amazing number of games, the participants are not even aware of this difference. Even when participants are explicitly asked to simulate expected real behavior or to optimize behavior, it is very doubtful whether the instructions have much significance for them. The results of many strategic games show how difficult it is for participants to distinguish between should and will. And the importance of strategic games as a method of strategic studies increases the role of this fallacy.

I do not mean to imply that there are many illusions on the influence of moral codes on international behavior among serious strategic analysts, (though such misbeliefs are widespread in the much larger groups of amateurs who regard themselves as qualified to judge strategic matters). Furthermore, the self-fulfilling and positive effects of this fallacy (on oneself and others) must be taken into account—expectations sometimes exert significant impact on behavior. When we speak about interaction between individuals, the behavior-influencing effect of expectations is well supported by empiric studies. Insofar as relations between nations take place through interpersonal interaction, we can expect strategic expectations to have an influence on behavior. Therefore, this fallacy can sometimes have a real impact on reality.

Nevertheless, its dangers are very serious. In particular, this fallacy leads one to ignore possibilities of radically undesirable behavior, since there is an underlying tendency to increase the subjective probability of those happenings which one regards as more desirable. (Again, the importance of subjective probabilities as a method of strategic studies reinforces the significance of this fallacy). This may not apply equally to all aspects of expectations. For instance, if one regards the Soviet Union as very aggressive, one will tend to include aggression among expected behavior. Even this may often be more a profession of principle than an operational characteristic of predictions; the few predictions of the dispatch of Soviet pilots to the United Arab Republic (even among the more hawkish analysts) is a case in point. Even, given that one expects a certain adversary to behave in an aggressive and undesirable way in some respects, one still tends to project onto him features one regards as desirable in other matters. For instance, once cost-benefit analysis became an accepted technique in the United States, there was a strong tendency to explain and predict behavior of adversaries as if they should, and therefore would, use cost-benefit analysis in their own decision-making processes.

It is especially hard—because of this (and other) fallacies—to expect a government to behave in ways which clearly contradict the long-term material interests of that government itself—for instance, in an extreme case, suicidal behavior, or, in less extreme cases, readiness to pay a high price and make large sacrifices for an ideology, a dogma, or a sense of national commitment.

Fallacy 3—Conflict is Stylized

When reading about war in the Middle Ages, we tend to be amazed. The rigid stylization of combat and the scarcity of military innovators who broke through accepted rituals of conflict and achieved victory by inventing new conflict patterns is surprising. It is much harder to adopt a similarly detached view of our own behavior. But, when we do adopt a distant view of contemporary events, then the stylized nature of our contemporary conflict behavior on the strategic level becomes visible. Stylized patterns of conflict go far beyond the rules of morals. They include the whole range of possible military and strategic actions. Especially constrained—and, therefore, ignored—are possible deviations which are, rightly so, branded as barbarian when someone tries them out. Systematic assassination of leaders, clandestine and anonymous delivery of nuclear bombs, poisoning of food and water, usage of hostages to achieve political aims—these are only a few of many possible patterns of behavior outside accepted styles of conflict (and contrary to accepted morality) and, therefore, universally condemned, usually avoided, and nearly never seriously considered and prepared for. With the development of technology, many additional, fargoing possibilities for counteraccepted conflict behavior became possible—making their nonconsideration all the more risky.

The fallacy does not lie in branding much of such possible behavior as inhuman and condemning it as such. The fallacy lies in the assumption—closely related to Fallacies 1 and 2 and based on a misreading of history—that the fact that counterstylized conflict behavior is avoided and condemned assures that such behavior will not occur. By neglecting to think of such possibilities, we create a dangerous risk of being unprepared if and when such behavior is resorted to by counterconventional actors and multiactors—including obviously, crazy states.

There is a cost to consideration of taboo behavior, including some increased probability that such behavior may occur, because attention is drawn to the feasibility and, sometimes, efficiency of such behavior and because the taboo may be reduced. But there is an even greater cost to ignoring it. Regarding the unthinkable as not worth thinking about because it is really unthinkable—this is the risky implication and the dangerous result of Fallacy 3. Again, this fallacy is more widespread among amateur strategists than among the professionals. This is illustrated, for instance, by opinions on preparation for, or, to be more exact, preparation against, possible biochemical warfare—not as something to be desired, but as something which has to be considered as within the realm of the possible, though, hopefully, improbable. Many possibilities of crazy behavior to be discussed in this book are ignored because of Fallacy 3. Even when some occur, they are treated as limited cases and not as indicators that much more crazy patterns of conflict may be in the making.

Not only are possibilities of counterstylistic behavior by adversaries ignored; but the possible benefits of engaging onself from time to time in counterstylistic behavior, of course within the boundaries of basic values, do not receive necessary attention. Fixation on stylistic conventions, therefore, inhibits innovation and though, on one hand, it prevents many undesirable activities, it also hinders, on the other hand, some desirable breakthroughs (including, for instance, counterstylistic disarmament and peacekeeping alternatives). The most risky situation is one where an adversary adopts counterstylistic patterns of conflict while oneself is bound by stylistic rigidity. If such an adversary adds significant action capabilities to this counterstylistic innovations, then, indeed, there is serious trouble. We shall see that this is well illustrated by the problem of crazy states.

Fallacy 4—Crisis Is Bad

A widespread view of crisis as always bad, as something that should be managed, reduced, and quieted down as soon as possible—is another interesting fallacy of United States strategic studies. By definition, crisis is any unexpected and more than incremental change in the situation, or in our perception of the situation. Since it is a time of accelerated change, crisis does increase the probability of undesired consequences; but, simultaneously, it often provides an opportunity to achieve desired objectives because of the loosening of the *status quo*. From the point of view of a different tacit theory, crisis can be regarded as an opportunity—and can even be initiated or instigated. In other words, instead of crisis management, crisis initiation and crisis utilization may be preferable.

The fallacy here is a double one: (a) crisis is not regarded as something to be initiated and utilized and, therefore, one does not expect the adversary to deliberately provoke a crisis; and (b) one avoids initiating a crisis, and, therefore, ignores a possibly important strategic instrument.

In both these respects, this fallacy is risky, though one must also recognize that by reducing the number of crises, risks often also get reduced.

Fallacy 5—The Adversary Is a Person

Personification of organization and interorganizational systems is a well-recognized mistaken tendency of the human mind. Regarding nations as if they were individuals is an even greater mistake, but nevertheless, a widespread one. Again, games illustrate this fallacy at work. Even when a country is represented by a small group, it is completely misleading to transpose the small groups' dynamics to the multidimensional bureaucracies and other social units, which constitute the country's policy-shaping cluster.[5] But this fallacy continues to be very powerful in most published strategic studies.

Fallacy 6—Adversaries Are Fixed

The view of an adversary as a unitary entity is related to Fallacy 6, which regards adversaries as not susceptible to change by our actions. Strategic literature does deal with influencing the behavior of an adversary—deterring him, getting him involved in alliances, supplying him with additional capacities, and so forth. But his inner characteristics and decision patterns are usually regarded as beyond our influence. The main characteristics of his society, of his values, and of his intent, are regarded as changing with time, but they are not usually regarded as targets for strategic action on our part.

This fallacy is less consistently held than some of the others. Foreign aid, for instance, is sometimes tied in with an awareness of possibilities to change the inner nature of international multiactors, as are cultural exchanges and a variety of political and economic activities. Furthermore, in considering strategic alternatives, impact on internal power struggles is sometimes taken into account. Nevertheless, possibilities to initiate change in the internal characteristics of adversaries are amazingly neglected in strategic studies—perhaps because of the still widespread tendency of such studies to look at strategic issues as if they are divorced from internal politics and society. This may, in some degree, be also a result of the doctrine of sovereignty, which prohibits action designed to influence someone else and which still exerts an amazing dominance over our world view. Whatever the genesis of this fallacy, it becomes particularly dangerous when internal developments in a country make it a major threat, for instance, when it becomes more and more crazy.

*Fallacy 7—Strategic Policy Is Separate
from Domestic Policies*

In political science, the interdependencies between domestic politics and foreign and strategic policies are well recognized and quite intensely studied under the concept of linkage politics.[6] This theorem, fully supported by current political experience, has had, as yet, little impact on strategic studies. Also, because of this fallacy, we seldom recognize the dependency of an adversary's strategy on his internal politics. (Even more surprising, sometimes strategic analysts know little about the domestic politics of the country where the study is going on.) This is the subject of Fallacy 7.

There are a number of legitimate reasons why strategic analysts are ignorant of domestic politics, including the following factors.

(a) In the past, most work on strategic problems was done in the military, which was inhibited and prohibited from considering domestic politics as a legitimate area for study, much less influencing it. This tradition maintained itself—even though many strategic analysts are civilians who in no way belong to the military profession.

(b) Especially abhorrent to democratic morality is the idea of using external activities for domestic political purposes. Once interdependence between domestic politics and strategic activities is recognized, the idea of not only adjusting strategic activities to domestic politics but of using strategic activities to actively influence domestic politics is too obvious to be comfortable. Therefore, resistance to including domestic politics within strategic studies is deeply rooted in important tenets of democracy.

(c) In a simpler world, domestic political goals of strategy were rather obvious and therefore seemed to need no specific consideration.

(d) Until quite recently, domestic politics in the United States could be taken more or less for granted with little expectation that internal changes would have significant impact on strategic policies. This was especially true because of the American belief that military affairs should be kept out of politics and the tendency to object to purely military activities to achieve mainly political goals (as illustrated in American World War II policies when, after the invasion of Europe, the decision was made to open the second front on the European west coast).

(e) Reliable methodologies for tying in strategic studies with domestic politics have been, until recently, unavailable, reinforcing the desire to ignore what cannot be well handled.

However justified some of the reasons for trying to keep strategic studies apart from the study of domestic politics may be, this dichotomy is no longer viable, as strongly brought out by developments in the United States. Therefore, this fallacy is very harmful. It inhibits the feasibility testing of strategic alternatives in terms of domestic politics, and the consideration of domestic political costs of different strategic alternatives.

Another harmful effect is the tendency to ignore the impact of domestic politics of a country on the adversaries of that country. Thus, for instance, deterrence is usually considered in terms of American capabilities and credibility, with credibility analyzed as resulting from American capabilities, external actions, and declarations by official leadership. The possibility that adversaries may interpret United States deterrence credibility and other aspects of strategic credibility on the basis of American domestic political developments is one which is usually not studied by analysts or considered by political actors. Certainly, strategic analysts are duty-bound to consider such factors and to make domestic political actors aware of the implications of domestic political behavior for American strategic policies—and for the strategic policies of other multi-actors, including adversaries.

Fallacy 8—Political Goals Are beyond
Strategic Analysis

This one single most important fallacy is also related to political aspects, namely, the political goals of security strategies. This is the fallacy that political goals of strategy are themselves beyond the domain of strategic studies.

This fallacy takes a variety of forms, beginning with the adoption of military aims (such as destroy the enemy's forces or occupy strategic territory) as political goals for strategies, and concluding with adoption of nonoperational concepts (such as preserve national security, deter the enemy or assure the status quo) as political goals for strategy. It is possible to discern some attempts to overcome this fallacy, but those are just in their beginnings.[h] Furthermore, insofar as known, the suspicion seems supported that war plans lack plausible tie-in to broader political objectives. The gulf between military planning and political objectives is well demonstrated by the contrast between detailed planning for the start of hostilities and their first stages, and the lack of thought about modes for terminating conflict in ways which achieve political objectives.[7]

This fallacy is deeply rooted in already mentioned rigid organizational reality. War planning is in the hands of the armed forces, the general staffs of which often achieve an advanced technical level of military operations planning. But military general staffs are politically and ideologically inhibited from dealing with political goals and are not equipped with the knowledge, staff and techniques for doing so. At the same time, Departments of State, while formally responsible for formulating long-range political goals, are distinguished in all

---

[h]Thus, in the United States, the *Annual Statement of the Secretary of Defense* and the new Annual Presidential Statement on *U.S. Foreign Policy* are far from being integrated, though in the 1971 versions, an increased interface can be discerned.

countries by their preoccupation with diplomacy—with emphasis on pragmatic bargaining with the representatives of other countries and rejection to foreign policy planning and intellectual analysis of political goals.

The National Security Council, especially under Henry Kissinger, represents an important attempt to overcome this fundamental weakness, as did at some periods the attempts to set up a Policy Planning Staff in the Department of State. New methods of policy analysis are now available, which do provide some of the intellectual tools that might permit better integration of strategic studies with consideration of political goals. But as yet, such integration has not been achieved, so that the fallacy still describes most strategic studies and strategic policy-making activities.

Fallacy 9—What Is Good for the United States Is
Good for All Others . . . Up to a Certain Point

Fallacy 9 is the first in a series of fallacies which can be reduced, with some simplification, to what I call the convex mirror effect. This is the tendency to regard a country as a miniature—or distorted version—of the United States (or developing in that direction). It is this tacit theory that other countries are similar to the United States—or are going to become similar once they get civilized and modernized—which is one of the main explanations for Fallacies 9 to 18. (In some countries, there operates the opposite fallacy, namely, that some adversaries are fundamentally and irreversably different; but this fallacy is not very important in American strategic studies.)

Fallacy 9 deals with a relatively minor aspect of this convex mirror effect, namely, the tendency to regard military doctrines and equipment which are good for the United States as good for others also, up to a certain point. The following fallacies deal with other, and, in some respects, more serious implications of this same convex mirror effect.

The best illustrations of Fallacy 8 relates to weapons. United States policy, when desiring to strengthen the armed forces of some friendly nation, is to help that nation to build up its armed forces—usually, in the pattern of the United States Army and equipped with United States weapons. The possibility that United States military structures, military doctrines, and military equipment may not fit the conditions and needs of other countries has little acceptance in the United States military. This possibility finds also little expression in the more pragmatic aspects of military aid. Thus, the fact that very little production in the United States and, until very recently, almost no research and development is directed toward developing weapons specifically tailormade for the needs of underdeveloped countries is a rather striking demonstration of this fallacy. This contradiction between absence of special efforts to design military doctrines, organizations, and equipment fitting other countries and their real needs is all the more amazing because it so strongly and frontally contradicts the Nixon Doctrine, which in principle aims at making friendly countries able to defend themselves.

In considering this fallacy, two additional points should be noted.

(1) Many countries want to receive weapons, even if ill-fitting for their real needs; what the United States tries to offer them instead is not modern equipment tailormade for the needs of the relevant country, but outdated United States-oriented and produced weapons systems.

(2) Much military aid also serves domestic political bureaucratic and economic purposes, both in the aid-giving and in the aid-receiving countries. Such needs may be satisfied by types of aid which do not fit any strategic requirements of the receiving countries.

But the fallacy that what is good for the United States is good for all others holds only up to a certain point. Beyond that point, what is good for the United States is regarded as bad for other countries. This point of sudden differentiation is most obvious in respect to nuclear weapons. The belief that nuclear weapons are bad for other countries and that nuclear proliferation is not only bad for the United States and bad for the world, but also for the proliferating countries, is widely accepted in most of the American strategic studies. The short shrift given to the different opinions of foreign strategic analysts demonstrates the strength of the second part of Fallacy 9.[i] There are some signs of second thoughts in recent American strategic studies, but those are a minority which, as yet, do not influence the mainstream of analyses and policy. Instead, there is a significant effort toward proving (or trying to prove) to other countries that nuclear weapons are bad for them and recommending that they build up their conventional forces—in the form of a miniature United States Army—never mind their local needs and conditions.

Furthermore, because of this fallacy, combined with Fallacy 2, other countries are not really expected to produce nuclear weapons. Even if, on the

[i]The insufficiencies of reasons given for the United States position that nuclear weapons are bad for other countries demonstrate Fallacy 6, but do not imply that nuclear weapons are necessarily useful for other countries. In the following chapter, I will examine some aspects of that issue, Even when nuclear weapons may be useful for some countries under some conditions, this does not contradict the need to prevent such countries from actually having nuclear weapons, because of United States or global interests (which, in turn, may or may not coincide). In Chapter 6, I discuss some cases in which countries should be prevented from developing nuclear weapons, not in order to serve their goals and not on the basis of *a priori* fallacious opinion—but in order to protect global and United States interests which, in those cases, happen to be identical.

intellectual level, some countries are expected to do so—this is not really accepted as a potential fact. As a result, very few United States strategic studies deal seriously with the implications of possible further nuclear proliferation.

In a more diffuse form, Fallacy 9 tends to take the form that global interests and the interests of mankind are identical with United States interests. Many illustrations are provided by studies dealing with the agreement to stop atmospheric testing of nuclear weapons. Even stronger illustrations are provided by strategic studies on the nonproliferation treaties, where distinctions between global and panhuman interests and American interests are conspicuous by their absence. This is not the result of a noble decision to subordinate United States interests to broader interests after the difference between those two is recognized. Instead, it is the result of a fuzzy underlying assumption that these two interests are identical.

Fallacy 10—Everyone Wants What We Want

The assumption that every country wants for itself what the United States wants (or, more correctly, apparently wanted in the past) is a most insidious fallacy, with various consequences in respect to misunderstanding of other actors, multiactors and adversaries. (Of course, the opposite assumption would be even more of a fallacy.) Related to this fallacy is its secondary version; namely, that those who do not want, as yet, what the United States wants will change their minds once they become developed.

The substantive content of the goals of other multiactors are perceived to be reasonable by United States traditional concepts, including, especially, rule of law, individual rights, personal freedom, individualistic material goods, economic advancement in terms of growing GNP, somewhat pragmatic attitudes, and a diffuse belief in the goodness of human beings. The fallacy that everyone wants what the United States wanted covers also a number of basic attitudes, but those are so important as to warrant discussion as separate fallacies.

The tendency to interpret the actions of others as ultimately directed at such goals is not universal. From time to time, some countries are recognized as having different goals; but the tendency is to limit such recognition to only very obvious cases. Even when other goals are recognized as dominating the behavior and culture of a country, this recognition is not accompanied by real understanding of what, for instance, an aggressive ideology implies and means for those who believe in it. Maybe this is going to change with the development in the United States, itself, of a number of aggressive ideologies. But, in general, absence of personal experience and direct exposure to other types of value systems inhibits and hinders correct appreciation of the possibilities and significance of other types of goals and ideologies. This is illustrated, to some extent, by the differences in tone in the literature written by those who had been exposed to Nazi activities and ideologies, and those who treated it from a distance.

Difficulty in handling ideologies radically different from United States values is also reflected in utility theories and the favorite conception of Pareto Optimality,[j] which is widely used in the United States (and elsewhere) as if it really expressed universal patterns of human values. Thus, rigid ideologies (where no trade-offs are possible and beliefs require others to be worse off) are not considered. The fact that it is in the United States that so-called economic theories of democracy have developed[8] (based on rational models of individuals with goals that can be compared—explicitly or implicitly—to economy goals) is an important symptom of the acceptance of this fallacy in the United States.

In particular, on the strategic level, this fallacy inhibits the recognition of ideologies which are directed at aggression, at forceful conversion of others, at breaking down of existing institutions, at transcendental and metaphysical objectives, and at similar, by traditional American culture, unreasonable goals—as will be illustrated in the concept of crazy states.

Fallacy 11–Development Will Help

Fallacy 10 is supplemented by Fallacy 11, which expresses the expectation that those who are not yet similar to the United States in goals (and some other characteristics discussed in the following fallacies), will become so once they are more developed. Given enough time, given economic progress, given a friendly hand and lack of provocation, and given exposure to United States culture—other countries will become civilized, in the sense of being more similar to the United States, including, in particular, its goal structure.

The fallacious nature of this assumption is becoming increasingly recognized. The idea that development may be accompanied by revolutionary ferment and a lot of internal and external aggressiveness is familiar in recent literature; furthermore, internal turmoil in the United States casts doubts on the expectation of reasonableness in respect to developed societies. But those hedgings of the fallacy are weak ones. Thus, in much of the literature on development, the unavoidability of a period of turmoil after development starts is recognized, although this period of unrest is usually regarded as temporary. Once development is really accomplished, turmoil is expected to pass away as snow under hot rays of sun, and reasonable countries are expected to emerge from the cocoons of immature aggressiveness.

---

[j]*Pareto Optimality* postulates that a situation is optimal when it is impossible to improve the payoffs to anyone without reducing them by a larger amount to someone else.[9]

This fallacy is very disturbing because it is a pleasant and optimistic belief—to shatter it may appear an inhuman act. Furthermore, as this fallacy serves as one of the main supporting arguments for foreign aid, to undermine it is again unpleasant because it may appear to negate some justifications for providing other countries with help. (Though the fallacy and its negation are irrelevant to moral reasons for helping others.) But, please note that I do not claim the zero hypothesis. I do not say that development necessarily leads to results which are unreasonable in terms of United States' (or global) humanistic values. I am only saying that the belief that development will automatically result in such values is an incorrect one: in some cases, development may lead to such values; in other cases, not. It is the blind opinion that development always, or usually, leads to reasonable United States-like goals which is a mistaken one and which, therefore, constitutes a misleading fallacy. (This opinion also inhibits search for novel forms of aid which really increase the probability of development in countries evolving in reasonable directions.)

Fallacy 12—Power Breeds Responsibility

A special form of Fallacy 11 is Fallacy 12, namely, that power breeds responsibility. It relates, in particular, to the strategic literature on proliferation of nuclear weapons. While most of the American literature is strictly opposed to such proliferation (or perhaps because it is strictly opposed to such proliferation), it tends to write off the risks involved in the nuclear capacities of countries which already have nuclear weapons. Also, in those few writings which do take seriously the possibilities of nuclear proliferation, the tendency is to regard such prospects of proliferation with distaste, but to reduce the danger by the assumption that the possession of nuclear weapons will breed more maturity and responsibilities—maturity and responsibility being understood as reasonable goals and precepts for behavior—that is, for behavior similar to that of the United States.

This fallacy is a good illustration of the strength of underlying tacit theories, because it has so little foundation in history or in any scientific theory of human behavior. Thus, there are no historic illustrations of usable weapons which have not been used at least several times. I agree—as pointed out in Fallacy 1—that history is no guide for the future. But if one should not say that what has happened will happen, there is even less reason to say that what has happened will never happen in the future. In all respects, the assumption that possession of powerful instruments educates one to a more responsible use of them is a doubtful one, especially when "responsible" is understood in its United States and Western cultural meaning. Again, this is a fallacy to be exposed through the construction of the crazy state concept.

Fallacy 13—Risk Is Minimized

Attitudes to risk are a main policy guideline,[k] underlying broad clusters of policies. The degree to which one is ready to bear risks and the extent to which one tries to play for lower risks or higher security levels (minimax or maximin) on one hand, or for higher possible achievements with some disregard for risks (maximax) on the other hand, or even to prefer high risks as a positive value in themselves—is an important and even critical factor in respect to strategic policies. The contemporary United States, for reasons which go beyond this book but which seem to be deeply rooted in American culture, tends to a minimization of risk policy. Preference for low-risk alternatives and a general tendency to avoid risky strategic initiatives are among the more important manifestations of this policy dimension in American strategic studies and activities.

In line with the general tendency to view others in a convex mirror fashion, the general assumption in United States strategic studies is that others follow the same megapolicies it does; that is, that others also try to reduce risks. The possibility of what in the United States is called reckless behavior, brinkmanship, and adventurism, is thus discounted. Those very terms, which are in widespread use as derogatory referents to high-risk behavior, are, themselves, expressions of this fallacy because the question of what one regards as reckless and what one regards as brinkmanship are, after all, value issues—the preferability of low-risk behavior being a matter of subjective preference and not one of scientific rationality in any correct sense of the term. Even in terms of expected average value, reduction of risk is not always a preferable strategy and the concept of expected average value, itself, is bound by a number of value assumptions.[10] A belief "give me victory of give me death" or "let me perish with the Philistines" presents different attitudes, hard to comprehend by American strategic studies and usually neglected in them. The concept of the crazy state will put into stark relief the dangers of this fallacy—inhibiting recognition of possible behavior by others.

Fallacy 14—Everyone Plays It Cool

The fallacy that everyone plays it cool is also related to the convex mirror tacit theory, but is completely different from those dealt with in Fallacies 12 and 13. This fallacy states that behavior is and will be calculated and clinically shaped by analysis, never mind the circumstances.

This fallacy is held both in respect to the United States and in respect to other international multiactors. International relations scholars with a broad

---

[k]Such policy guidelines can be regarded as master policies or as megapolicies which are an underlying principle for series of more specific policies.[11]

background in history and social sciences are aware of the fallacious nature of this assumption and have often warned against it. But still, this fallacy is accepted in many strategic studies (at least implicitly), perhaps because it reflects the mental processes and professional symbols of strategic analysts, themselves, and because it permits refinement of sophisticated conflict models and strategic policy tools (which break down unless the assumption that crises are played out clinically and quite coldly is accepted).

Good illustrations of this fallacy in operation are various escalation ladders, city exchange models, limited nuclear war between the major power scenarios, and various novel strategic ideas such as demonstration nuclear blasts as communication symbols *vis-a-vis* major adversaries. On a broader level beyond professional strategic analysts, the widespread neglect of total-war possibilities, of sudden nuclear attacks by the major adversaries, and of civil defense activities, and some of the opposition to ABM are symptoms of this fallacy.

This fallacy is not based on the fact that cool and calculated behavior is regarded as one of the possible assumptions considered by strategic studies, but on the fact that it is a nearly exclusive assumption underlying many strategic studies. Calculated and cool behavior, even under the extreme situations of a limited nuclear clash between the two supercountries, is a possibility. But there is a world of difference between regarding this as one of the possibilities and regarding it as the most probable or only possibility. Even when looking on the United States in the future, the assumption that one can be sure that the supreme United States policy-makers will behave analytically if confronted by a strong nuclear provocation by the Soviet Union cannot be relied upon. Even less can such assumptions be relied upon in respect to other countries, which, for a variety of reasons, may be even more prone to spasm reactions.

The question is not limited to the two supercountries. Spasm reactions by other countries, when those countries have significant external-action capabilities, may be highly significant for the United States—and for the world as a whole. Therefore, even if in respect to the Soviet Union and the United States one has good reason to expect cool behavior (and this is doubtful), there is less reason for such expectations in respect to some other countries which are passing through intense turmoil. Neglect of the possibility of spasm reaction by some international multiactor who has serious damaging capabilities is one of the amazing neglects in many contemporary American strategic studies—(with the exception of some of the studies dealing with nuclear proliferation, where possible spasm reaction by another multiactor is a main argument for inhibiting such proliferation)—and one which potentially can cause tragedy and even catastrophe.

Fallacy 15—Means Serve Ends

More general in scope than Fallacy 14 is Fallacy 15, which presumes rationality (in the correct meaning of the term; namely, that means are positively related to ends). The assumption here is a double one: (a) that means are not arbitrary, in the sense of constituting subjective behavior unrelated to any ends, such as purely cathartic behavior or essentially random action; and (b) that means are related to ends in a way which we regard as objectively justified in terms of positivistic philosophy (even though, of course, not necessarily correct). Thus, for instance, astrology, even while subjectively claiming to relate means to ends, is regarded by us as objectively unjustified and, therefore, irrational.

In this fallacy, the assumptions are that there exist some identified relations between means and ends and that international actors and multiactors operate according to prescriptions based on such relations. More extreme and nevertheless widely accepted in strategic studies is the image that international multiactors decide on their activities with the help of some benefit-cost framework. Means clearly unrelated to ends are regarded as miscalculations (rather than as expressions of a system which runs by different principles). For instance, behavior dictated by detailed dogma which does not positively tie in particular acts to explicated goals is a stranger to this mode of thinking. This fallacy is quite a straitjacket for the prediction of strategic contingencies and for efforts to shape them.

Fallacy 16—Negotiations Help

Fallacy 16 (and also the next two fallacies), is again derived from the fundamental tendency to view others in a mirror of oneself. But it is different in direction from the last few fallacies—though based in part on them.

Fallacy 16 is related to a widespread American belief in negotiations, which, in turn, is closely related to the belief that others are reasonable. It is based on (1) expectation of a common interest; (2) a preference for compromise projected on the other participants; (3) on the already-mentioned desire to avoid crisis; and (4) on the general expectation that reasonable parties can always agree on something which is in the interest of all of them. It is assumed that there exists some potential point of agreement which makes all participants better off and, on which, therefore, they will agree—if only the common interest is clarified, suspicion is discarded, and the real interests of the parties are explicated. (These expectations are typical for lawyers—who, in the United States and many other countries, are a main source of policy-makers.)

The United States as a negotiator reveals a number of additional fallacies, but these are well treated somewhere else[1] and, therefore, do not need additional discussion here. But, the very belief in negotiations as always useful is a fundamental fallacy in strategic studies.

Fallacy 17–Agreements Are Kept

Fallacy 17 should be kept separate from Fallacy 16. Fallacy 16 stated that negotiations are useful aside from possible achievement of an agreement or because they may lead to an agreement. Fallacy 17 focuses on the agreement itself, expressing the expectation that agreements make a difference because they are often kept. The historic incorrectness of the view that agreements are usually kept has been explored elsewhere and, therefore, need not occupy us here.[12] Sufficient to note that agreements per se have played only a limited and sometimes misleading role in shaping strategic reality—though, of course, one must also avoid the opposite fallacy, that agreements are never kept and have no practical consequences at all.

The dangers of this fallacy are illustrated by the neglect in strategic studies of discussion of possible contingencies if major agreements on strategic issues should be violated. For instance, the nonproliferation treaty leaves quite open and unsolved the question, what if one of the sides is discovered as not keeping the agreement—something that may be so unexpected and so unpleasant as to cause the inspection machinery to try to avoid detection of swindling. Strategic arms limitations pose similar issues, if one expects agreements often to be broken. On quite a number of issues, if agreements are not expected to be kept, some other form of accommodation rather than an explicit and formalized agreement may be preferable. But a possibly productive line of thinking is inhibited because of Fallacy 17.

Fallacy 18–World Opinion Is Real/Unreal

Fallacy 18 deals with the tendency to jump to one of two extremes, each one of which is erroneous and constitutes a fallacy: on one hand, a belief that world opinion exists and that it makes a real difference to strategic problems; on the other hand, a belief that world opinion does not exist and that it has no significance whatsoever for strategic problems.

---

[1]Thus, Fred C. Ikle identified five main American shortcomings in negotiating with Communist powers: excessive attention to ephemeral rhetoric, pettifoggery, succumbing to semantic infiltration, treating Soviet evaluations as immutable, and misjudging changes in our own values.[13]

In its positive form—that world opinion is real and matters a lot—this fallacy is rooted in a positive view of the world as cast largely in the image of oneself, and is based through the convex mirror theory on an image and ideology which allocates a lot of weight to public opinion in the United States itself. In this version, this fallacy relies on world public opinion to have real impact on international behavior, including prevention of some very unpleasant contingencies. It implies that potential aggressors will be deterred by world opinion, that agreements will be enforced by world opinion, and that world opinion which favors the United States is an asset worth paying for by giving up policies which otherwise may be preferable.

In its negative form—that world opinion is a mirage and does not matter at all—the assumption is that strategic reality is shaped by objective factors and/or by decisions of individuals who ignore world opinion. It implies that world opinion has no impact whatsoever on strategic reality and that its cultivation is not worth any costs.

In both its forms, this is a significant fallacy, as only very few strategic studies (and strategic policies) seem to be able to adopt a balanced position between these two incorrect extremes.

Summary

The 18 fallacies briefly sketched in this chapter are not universally shared, as already noted. Also, the list of 18 fallacies is not complete. Many other fallacies are widespread in strategic studies.[14] But these are the fallacies most salient to the crazy state issue. Because of the important impact of these fallacies on actual international behavior and real strategic issues, their exposure (or, at least, encouragement of insights into their existence as the result of one tacit theory which coexists with others which should also be taken into account)—is among the main potential contributions to strategic analysis and policy of study of the crazy states problem. These fallacies are, therefore, both a background for a treatment of crazy states and an object for them: in part, neglect of the crazy states problem results from these fallacies. And reduction of the hold which these fallacies have over strategic studies in the United States and in other countries is one of the main goals of this study.

2 The Concept of Crazy States

The concept of crazy states as defined by me is critical for my analysis. It contradicts most of common sense, many accepted perceptions, widespread expectations and, in particular, nearly all of the strategic fallacies discussed in Chapter 1. It also somewhat differs from the meanings of the term crazy as used in common discourse or in psychology. Therefore, the concept of crazy states must be carefully considered.

Aggressive religious movements such as the Christian Crusaders or the Islam Holy Warriors; anarchists after the First World War and before it; contemporary terrorist groups in the United States, in Canada, in the Middle East, and in some South American countries; Nazi Germany; and—to a more limited extent—Japan before the Second World War—these are some illustrations of what I call crazy states. While, for the purposes of this book, a small number of prototype[a] constructs serve as main subjects for analysis, nevertheless the prototypes must meet the variety of historical reality and of future potential realization. This precludes any simple conception of crazy states. Rather, the concept of craziness must be broken down into several dimensions and a number of prototypes must be constructed on the basis of different combinations of those dimensions. In this way, an initial set of different prototypes of crazy states can be arrived at, some of which have been approximated by historical reality, and some of which have some probability of approximated realization in the future.

Before taking up construction of these prototypes, I want to point out my value—free use of the term crazy states—a term which I use as a technical concept, as defined and explained in this chapter.[b] While the constructed and discussed prototypes are by contemporary Western culture and United States culture in particular, crazy, this is a culturally given and timebound value

---

[a]From a methodological point of view, these prototypes are pure types or ideal types, as used by Max Weber.

[b]Alternative concepts which I could have used are fanatic state, extreme state, ideologically aggressive state, missionary state, terror state, etc. Each one of these terms and other possible concepts would be open to misunderstanding, as is the concept of crazy states itself. One possibility was to coin a new term, such as X-type state, but this would have made this book hard to read and even more abstract than it is. The reader is strongly urged to try to keep in mind my exposition of the meaning of craziness as used in this book—a meaning somewhat different from common usage of the term. Thus, as will be explained later, a crazy state can behave rationally in the instrumental sense, that is, it can pick instruments which are highly effective for achievement of its (crazy) goals.

judgment. Viewed from a perspective of one or another crazy state, the United States would be discussed and analyzed in terms of supercrazy features and behaviors. From some moral points of view, some may in fact regard one or another of the crazy prototypes as superior to the United States: readiness to sacrifice oneself and to take high risks for collectively shared and believed in values, may appear to some as morally superior to looking after individual goals, abstract rules of law and achievement of a well-adjusted life of aggregation of material goods and routinized relations with other individuals, who are equally missing deep commitment to collective transcendental values. To make an even more extreme illustration, if someone deeply and sincerely believed that other people are better off dead than to live as nonbelievers, then one will be ready and indeed feel oneself obligated to kill others for deep moral purposes. In such a case, we have what I in this book call an extreme case of craziness, even though it may be accompanied by deep and sincere feelings of moral obligations which—were they only directed at some other goal and a different type of belief—we would all admire and respect very much.

Because of the subjective basis of all beliefs, intrinsic values, transcendental obligations and commitments, most of the dimensions by which some states are classified as crazy (or normal) are arbitrary from a scientific point of view. In order to avoid mixing up moral judgment with analytical discourse, I want to make this point absolutely clear. While I regard several types of crazy states as highly dangerous for the world and therefore recommend a number of countermeasures, including some extreme ones, this may or may not involve moral condemnation. We may understand a terrorist, sympathize with some of the reasons which brought about his present state, and sometimes even appreciate the moral purposes he may have in mind. Nevertheless, it may be necessary to make sure he cannot cause any damage.

Clarification of the concept of craziness as used in this book requires differentiation between five main dimensions as described below.[c]

Goal Contents. This quality can be expressed in various ways, ranging from official and semiofficial pronouncements by the leaders of a country to concrete types of behavior, and including various artifacts of culture and media, such as literature and drama, news reporting, and activities of youth organizations Within the strategic context, we are interested in goals which involve aggressive activities abroad (or, when the crazy state is a noncountry unit—aggressive activities against other groups). Such goals can range in content from slight revisions of the border up to conversion of the world to a new dogma.

I will use the terms reasonable, unreasonable, and counterreasonable as referent to the goal-contents dimension.

---

[c]All five dimensions can be regarded as parts of a multidimensional objective function, crazy states being characterized by the particular shape of their objective function.

Goal Commitment. No less important in some respects than the contents of goals is the intensity with which they are held, that is, the degree of goal commitment. This concept can be overrationalized in terms of the price that a state, as led by a given group, is willing to pay for achievement of those goals. Goal commitment can range in intensity from daydreaming to complete commitment, leading up to a readiness for martyrdom.

I will use the terms low intensity, medium intensity, and high intensity as referent to the goal-commitment dimension.

Risk Propensity. This quality is a dimension of particular importance for the concept of crazy states. Risk propensities may range from an extreme dislike of any risks, to a preference for low-risk policies, up to an extreme preference for taking high risks—regarded by American standards as recklessness and brinkmanship.[d]

I will use the terms low risk, medium risk, and high risk as referents to the risk-propensity dimension, while ignoring the negative extreme of strong fear of even minimum risk, which is abnormal in the opposite direction from crazy states.

Means-goals Relation. This dimension, as contrasted with all other dimensions here, has an objective criteria (if some metaphysical assumptions of positivistic philosophy are taken for granted). It is possible to make an objective judgment on how far given goals are served by certain means or not. We may lack the knowledge and information for making this judgment, but in principle, means-goals relation can be dealt with on the intellectual level. Therefore, it is sometimes possible to identify clearly counterproductive means and means based on absurd reasons (such as astrology, unless it is a randomizer or a cover for tacit knowledge in the absence of applicable objective criteria).

In addition to objective instrumental rationality, irrationality, and counterrationality, there may also be cases of subjective instrumental rationality, irrationality, and counterrationality. Subjective instrumental irrationality and counterrationality exist where the decision-makers do not even claim that any relations obtain between the means and the goals. Much as such a view may appear not only absurd but nearly impossible to persons brought up in Western culture, it is one which should not be ignored. Actions which are explicitly justified in terms of satisfying passing moods or which are represented proudly as taken under the influence of altered states of consciousness illustrate such a possibility. Actual cases of action not even nominally justified in terms of any means-goals relation are illustrated, for instance, by ritualistic killings committed

---

[d]It is important to note that risk propensity relates to the evaluation of risks *per se*, separate analytically from the expected value of particular outcomes.

under the influence of psychotic drugs. To avoid seemingly contradictory terms such as crazy rational states, I will use the terms instrumental, noninstrumental and counterinstrumental as referents to the means-goals relation dimension, including its objective and subjective facets.

Style. When we focus our intentions on style—as contrasted with goal contents, risk propensity and means-goals relation—it is possible to distinguish between two deviations relevant to the crazy states issue from what is regarded normal behavior within the international context. One deviation is a strong ritualistic-dogmatic fixation on specific types of behavior and expressions. It is a stylistic feature separate from goal contents, risk propensity, or means-goals relation. (Some Communist and Asian patterns of communication illustrate this stylistic feature and are hard for Western negotiators to understand.) The second deviation is the propensity and preference for stylistic innovations which are not bound by accepted opinions and which are not regulated by accepted patterns. Aircraft hijacking, taking diplomats as hostages, and selective assassinations—are illustrations of such stylistic innovations already in existence. Hypothetical illustrations are only limited by our imagination, by our inability to think of the unthinkable, and by the undesirability of supplying ideas to crazy states.[e] I will use the terms accepted, unaccepted, and counteraccepted—with or without the adjective ritualistic—as referents to the style dimension.

Possibilities for classification, subclassifications, fine distinctions, and subdistinctions in respect to all these dimensions of normality versus craziness are infinite. But elaboration of a detailed breakdown of the dimensions would be a pure exercise in taxonomy, which would detract rather than add to the basic line of analysis of this book. Analysis of the main problems of crazy states at the present state of study of this subject requires a few clear-cut prototypes rather than a range of shady distinctions. Therefore, I will limit myself to an ordinal three-step classification of these dimensions, as presented in Table 2-1.

These dimensions of craziness can be used for behavioral study of reality, that is, description and dissection of historic situations. It is possible to take real cases of crazy international behavior and analyze them in terms of dimensions. Thus, Nazi Germany, the Crusaders, Holy Wars, imperialistic states, terror groups, and so on can be classified, described, and analyzed with the help of the dimensions of craziness. Such an endeavor would be much more than an exercise in classification. It may provide better understanding of crazy states, permit inductive validation of general patterns and relationships, provide a basis for reliable predictions concerning the emergence of crazy states in the future and—ultimately—derivation of a theory of crazy states and modeling of their relationships with the environment.

---

[e]This is an important consideration which I confronted in writing this book. Because of it, I use illustrations more sparsely than would otherwise be desirable.

Table 2-1
Dimensions of Craziness

Dimensions	Degrees of Craziness		
	(1) Low	(2) Medium	(3) High
(a) Goal Contents	(1) Reasonable Status quo or minor external goals, such as: voluntary commercial trade activities; minor influence on policies of other states; no or very limited diffusion of ideology; no territorial change or very minor border adjustments.	(2) Unreasonable Extensive external goals, such as economic hegemony over other states; much control over some policies of other states; significant export of ideology; medium changes in borders.	(3) Counterreasonable Very extensive external goals, such as full control over economic activities of other states; full control of all policies of other states; total conversion of others to ideology; radical changes in borders, up to destruction of other states and absorption or liquidation of their population.
(b) Goal Commitment	(1) Low Intensity Devotion of minor parts of budget and limited manpower to external goals; no readiness to sacrifice internal goals for external goals.	(2) Medium Intensity Devotion of large parts of budget, GNP, and manpower to external goals; readiness to sacrifice internal goals for external goals.	(3) High Intensity Devotion of most of budget, GNP, and manpower to external goals; the internal goals regarded only as means for external goals; external goals accepted as national mission, up to readiness to sacrifice self-existence to achieve external goals.
(c) Risk Propensity	(1) Low Risk Strong tendency to reduce risks by avoiding risky policies.	(2) Medium Risk Acceptance of risk, with a mix between more risky and less risky policies.	(3) High Risk Preference for very risky policies, up to ideological commitment to adventurism and risk-taking as a preferable lifestyle.
(d) Means-Goals Relation	(1) Instrumental Full formal desire to be rational; justification of means in terms of goals; usually means do not obviously contradict goals; efforts to develop and use methodologies to improve means-goals relations (such as systems analysis, PPBS, and policy sciences); where easily usable criteria are available, means tend to fit goals.	(2) Noninstrumental Limited lip service to rationality; little justification of means in terms of goals; some means obviously contradict goals; no interest in means-goals relation-improving methodology; even where easily usable criteria are available, means often do not fit goals.	(3) Counterinstrumental Ideology completely ignores or rejects rationality; no justification of means in terms of goals; many means obviously contradict goals; explicit resistance to means-goals relation-improving methodology and explicit preference for nonrational methods, such as astrology and arbitrary leader myths; even where easily usable criteria are available, means very often do not fit goals.
(e) Style	(1) Accepted Nearly full compliance with present styles, even under provocation; some deviations themselves take place in stylized forms within special and isolated units, such as the CIA. Some elasticity, incremental change capacity, and adjustment to context.	(2) Unaccepted Much deviation from present styles, such as: extensive insurgence activities formally engaged in; some use of terror, execution of hostages, blackmail, sabotage, etc.; some unannounced use of biochemical weapons. Some elasticity, incremental change capacity, and adjustment to context.	(3) Counteraccepted Extreme deviation from present styles (and morals) such as: genocide (there as a style of operation, not as goal content); mass assassination of leaders; food poisoning; systematic sabotage of civilian peaceful facilities; countervalue terror against schools, hospitals, recreation areas, civil transportation, etc.; extensive killing of diplomats; full biochemical warfare. Some elasticity, incremental change capacity, and adjustment to context.
	(1a) Accepted Ritualistic Fixation and rigidity in respect to more or less accepted styles.	(2a) Unaccepted Ritualistic Fixation and rigidity in respect to specific unaccepted styles.	(3a) Counteraccepted Ritualistic Fixation and rigidity in respect to specific counteraccepted styles.

Note: As explained in the text, the classification is based on contemporary Western, and especially United States standards. Therefore, the classification is culture-bound and time-bound and does not presume any universal, absolute, or intrinsic validity.

However interesting and worthwhile such an endeavor may be, my approach in this book is different. For a definite treatment of crazy states which wants to arrive at general theories of such phenomena, historic study in which the dimensions of craziness are used as one of the conceptual tools, is essential. But for a policy-oriented exploration, a different utilization of the dimensions of craziness is preferable, namely, the synthesis of prototypes.

Hypothetically, different combinations of goals contents, goal commitments, risk propensity, means-goals relation, and styles may occur and form a large number of possible conditions. Some of these combinations may be less probable than others, and some may even appear to us, with present knowledge, to be impossible because of inherent contradictions—though this is an *a priori* assumption which should not be taken as completely reliable. By breaking down the dimensions into subdimensions and considering different possible mixes of subdimensions in respect to different issues within any one state, many more combinations can be made. But for purposes of analyzing crazy states and their strategic implications, a smaller number of sharper and more extreme prototypes is preferable. Reality will move on the ranges between the various prototypes, but for clarification of the basic issues involved, sharper and fewer prototypes are most useful. A set of main prototypes, based on combinations of the three-step scale, together with some initial comments on their features (to be elaborated in later chapters), is represented in Table 2-2. This set serves as a basis for my later discussion when these prototypes will be further developed and considered.

To complete initial circumscription of the concept of crazy states, we must now add the unit to which the various dimensions of craziness apply, that is, the societies and countries involved. These can be classified as (a) countries; and (b) noncountries. Most attention in strategic studies still goes to countries, and indeed, countries are the most important multiactor. But this was not always the case in the past and may not always be the case in the future. At different periods, multiactors which were not countries fulfilled critical strategic roles. Sufficient to mention the Catholic Church, moving nomads, medieval cities, and Chinese secret societies to illustrate the security implications on noncountry multiactors. In the future, with expected changes in weapons technology and possible changes in postsaturation societies, noncountry units may become more important as security issues than they are now (even on the international scene)—and thus they may become a main theme for strategic studies. This possibility begins to be recognized in the growing attention to what is called subversion, guerrilla warfare, internal warfare and international terrorism.

These phenomena involve subcountry units ranging from very small groups up to large movements, or even country-within-country structures. Less recognized are other noncountry multiactors, some of which are intercountry, and some of

Table 2-2
Main Prototypes of Craziness

	Combination of Dimensions				
(a) Goal Contents	(b) Goal Commitment	(c) Risk Propensity	(d) Means-Goals Relation	(e) Style	Name
Reasonable (1) some unreasonable (2)	Low intensity (1) some medium intensity (2)	Low risk (1), some medium risk (2)	Instrumental (1), some noninstrumental (2)	Accepted (1), some unaccepted (2) with or without some accepted ritualism (1a)	Normal state
Unreasonable (2)	Medium intensity (2)	Medium risk (2)	Instrumental (1), some noninstrumental (2)	Unaccepted (2), with or without some unaccepted ritualism (2a)	Somewhat crazy state
Counterreasonable (3)	High intensity (3)	Medium risk (2) and some high risk (3)	Instrumental (1), some noninstrumental (2)	Counteraccepted (3)	Crazy state
Counterreasonable (3)	High intensity (3)	Medium risk (2) and some high risk (3)	Counterinstrumental (3)	Counteraccepted (3)	Crazy noninstrumental state
Counterreasonable (3)	High intensity (3)	Medium risk (2) and some high risk (3)	Counterinstrumental (3)	Counteraccepted ritualistic (3a)	Crazy noninstrumental ritualistic state
Counterreasonable (3)	High intensity (3)	Extreme high risk (extreme 3)	Instrumental (1), some noninstrumental (2)	Counteraccepted (3)	Crazy martyr state
Counterreasonable (3)	High intensity (3)	Extreme high risk (extreme 3)	Counterinstrumental (3)	Counteraccepted (3) or counteraccepted ritualistic (3a)	Crazy noninstrumental martyr state

Note: This table presents only some possible combinations of dimensions of craziness (referred to by the numbers used in Table 2–1 above), with special attention to construction of prototypes of extreme crazy states.

which do not belong to any country at all. Units which cross national borders and have significant memberships in a number of countries, such as a religious movement or—as some times—the Communist movement, illustrate the case of intercountry units. Units which regard themselves as outside the domain of any existing country, such as some of the medieval orders and, nowadays, some of the Palestinian movements, illustrate the category of belonging-to-no-country units. I am including all these forms of multiactors which are not countries under the term noncountry units.

As I will show later, the strategic problems that may be posed by noncountry multiactors (and perhaps even by crazy individuals) may become growing ones—with such units becoming more probable and with their capacities to cause significant trouble being on the increase. For purposes of conceptual economy, I am including country, subcountry, and intercountry units within the concept of crazy states, using the double meaning of state as referring (a) to countries; and (b) to situations. Often, when speaking about crazy states, I refer mainly to crazy countries, as will be made clear by the context. But noncountry units are very important for the problem of states-of-craziness, and I will specifically consider and analyze them from time to time.

I will return to the classification of crazy states from the point of view of their external-action capabilities in Chapter 4. But before pursuing this task, the question must be faced whether crazy states are a possibility at all.

3 Probability of Crazy States

Policy analysis must be justified by more than intellectual curiosity and theoretical fascination. Therefore, before proceeding with our study of crazy states, we must demonstrate its significance for the real world. In other words, we must face the question, What are the probabilities of crazy states?

Even if crazy states have low probability, the study of them as a counterfactual construct (that is, a construct contradicting all known phenomena—though not theoretically impossible) would be beneficial. It could, for example, help repudiate the fallacies which result from the tacit theory of most American strategic studies (as discussed in Chapter 1) and thus help improve these studies on realistic issues. But I do not think that crazy states are counterfactual constructs; rather, I think they are possible future occurrences of history-shaping impact.

My reasons for this belief can be summed up in the following statements.

1. Crazy states have happened in the past. This at least, shows that they are possible in the sense that they do not contradict basic patterns of human and social behavior.
2. While present knowledge is too limited to allow us to construct a theory on the causes of crazy states, accelerated societal transformation—by definition—involves appearance of infrequent and even completely new, social phenomena. Some of the latter can be crazy states. Therefore, the contemporary rate of social change must be regarded as a factor which may contribute to the emergence of crazy states.
3. It is possible to diagnose a contemporary trend toward the emergence of crazy states. While they appear as isolated instances and mainly on the noncountry level, their imitation and diffusion may be encouraged by the characteristics of present mass communication which can reinforce underlying (and unknown) reasons and accelerate a possible trend toward craziness. Even if the present occurrences do not become as yet a trend, they may indicate the possibility of such a trend beginning in the future.
4. Historically, crazy states occurred from time to time. But many of them were localized and easily repressed. Modern technology changes this situation, permitting incipient crazy states both to (1) build up significant external-action capabilities; and (2) to achieve stature thanks to their fascination for

the mass media. These possibilities make crazy states more probable and more dangerous if realized.

Even adopting a conservative scientific position and assuming that we cannot know whether crazy states can happen and that we cannot know the probability of their happening—nevertheless, it is my conclusion that uncertainty in this matter justifies (a) close study; (b) contingency planning; and (c) constant monitoring of reality to identify early signs of actualization.

A fortiori, it is important to deal with the crazy states issue if we think that the realization of crazy states has a low but distinct probability. Therefore, I want to support my claim that not only can we not be sure that crazy states are impossible, but that there is a real case for assuming that crazy states are actually possible.

There exist no evidence-supported theories on the variables influencing the probability of the realization of crazy states; there exist no methods and data on which such a theory can at present be based (though in principle such data can be found and suitable methods can be designed); and no experience-based indicators are available, which permit reliable prediction of the probability of emergence of crazy states. Therefore, we must look for other methods for arriving at some impression, which is more than a pure guess, on the possibility of appearance of crazy states. Here, we must bear in mind that policy analysis is based on criteria different from those on which traditional science is built.

In policy analysis, we search for ways to improve decisions, so that even guesstimate is preferable to pure guess and careful impression is superior to arbitrary idiosyncrasy. In tradition science, much more rigorous quality control is necessary and possible, because one can always say "I don't know"—an answer which in respect to policy issues is appropriate only when findings are so doubtful as to make preferable decisions in which they are not at all considered. Therefore, the threshold of significance is much lower in policy analysis than it is in traditional sciences, though of course, the reliability of any policy analysis should be carefully monitored and explicated. These conclusions apply fully to strategic studies, where scientific knowledge is as yet very scarce, where critical decisions often cannot be delayed, and where, therefore, duly hedged low-validity policy analysis can be of much heuristic help for better policy-making.

Therefore, I think I am justified within the context of this study and with awareness of the weakness of that method, to utilize scenarios in order to consider the possibilities of crazy state realization. Scenarios consist of hypothetical series of events which connect the present to some alternative future. The more a scenario fits available knowledge and the more it correlates with observable phenomena and trends, the more useful it is as a technique of policy analysis, including strategic analysis. (Though its validity is on a different level than that of behavioral empiric research.) I will proceed by presenting a number of scenarios leading to the realization of crazy states. Clearly, these scenarios constitute no scientific proof and should not even serve as a basis for allocation of subjective probabilities. All that is claimed—and this is enough for my present limited purposes—is that the scenarios indicate a probability higher than zero that crazy states may be realized, and that the scenarios permit improved impressions on the significance of the crazy states issue.[1]

It is especially important, and very disturbing, to point out that crazy states are not only a possibility in remote corners of the world, but that they can also develop in highly modernized and advanced countries, including—under certain conditions which have a low probability, but one higher than zero—the United States and the Soviet Union. This is a possibility which should not look absurd to anyone who knows history. Germany, a highly civilized country in all respects before the Nazi regime, is one of the more extreme real-life instances. Especially because of the strategic implications of a superpower becoming a crazy state, this hypothetical possibility deserves special attention. Let me, therefore, start with two scenarios which put forth a possible evolution of the United States and the Soviet Union, respectively, into crazy states.

Scenario 1. United States Transformation into a Crazy State

Increasing turmoil, accompanied by rising levels of terror directed at public transportation, recreation areas, schools, public utilities, public officials, corporate directors, etc. Regular court systems and public order systems are unable to handle rising waves of terrorism, especially because of oscillation in public attitudes and the multiplicity of groups tending to extreme pacifism on one extreme and to intense violence on the other extreme. Consequently, an increase in level of public anxiety, accompanied by lynching of individuals suspected of participation in terrorist activities. Party leaders try to adopt a reasonable position, combining social reforms with traditional methods for handling public disturbances. A candidate capable of significant rhetoric and unusual television appeal emerges, sets up a new party machinery, presents an ideology based on public order and repression of dissent, and promises to make the world safe for the United States. In the meantime, the Soviet Union takes advantage of the crisis in the United States and makes aggressive moves in Europe, Asia, and the Middle East. Therefore, "making the world safe for the United States" more and more is associated with an intensely held ideology that direct defeat of the Soviet Union is essential for the United States' safety. After being elected as President, the new leader develops a highly centralized control system over nuclear weapons, while putting forth an ideology that steps must be taken to liquidate the military might of the Soviet Union as soon as possible. Internal oppression of minorities, of dissent, and of political opposition are accomplished by the declaration of martial law. The nuclear first-strike counterpopulation capability is reinforced, together with crash programs to develop new weapons able to destroy with a first strike the Soviet retaliatory arsenals. The manifest destiny of the United States to free the world—and itself—from the dangers of Communism is the major ideological declaration of the President and his followers.

Scenario 2. The Soviet Union Transforms into a Crazy State

Economic problems and demands for liberalization from youth, intellectuals, and the managerial elite, combined with anti-Russian movements in Hungary, Poland, Rumania, and Czechoslovakia, cause political turmoil in the leadership. There is demand for a return to a purer ideology with commitment to the classical ideas of Communism, namely, a classless world society led by the pioneer of Communism—the Soviet Union. A group of purists gains control of the central organs of the Communist Party and recruits supporters by promising a new faith and economic advancement. Efforts by some of the satellite countries to break away from the Warsaw Pact result in military intervention by the Soviet Union. The belief that communism and capitalism cannot coexist crystallizes. Strong internal turmoil in the United States and significant turmoil in Western Europe reinforce the image that Western capitalist societies are decadent and ripe for communism. The ideas that the Soviet Union must (1) prepare for a final war to end all wars; (2) overthrow capitalist society; and (3) make the world secure for communism are increasingly supported. There is rapprochement with China on the basis of this ideology and investments in all types of military capabilities are much increased. The leadership adopts the position that because of internal weaknesses, one massive strike at the command and control centers of the western world would finish capitalism. Preparations for a first strike directed mainly at political centers throughout the western world are discussed and the idea that it is necessary to liquidate the leaders of the western world so that their people will be free for communism is put forth.

These scenarios are only single illustrations from a much larger set of possible transformations.[2] The construction of a number of such scenarios does not imply that the transformation of the United States and/or the Soviet Union into a crazy state is highly probable. But insofar as the scenarios are not completely counterfactual, they at least demonstrate the possibility of such a transformation.

Table 3-1
Some Hypothetical Transformations of Present States into Crazy States

Present States	Transformation Phases	Resulting States of Craziness					
		Goal Contents	Goal Commitment	Risk Propensity	Means-Goals Relation	Style	Crazy State Prototype Approximated
South Africa	Neighboring black countries modernize, establish armies, adopt ideology to free their black brothers in South Africa, and organize terror activities directed at white population of South Africa. Majority in United Nations expels South Africa and enforces some embargo and widespread ostracism. A semireligious belief in their mission to save human civilization through assurance of white supremacy all around the world ascends in South Africa, gains dominance, and is feverishly believed in by leadership. Contacts with small groups with similar belief in Europe, America, and Australia are established, and a master plan to keep all nonwhite countries under control through nuclear threats is publicized. In South Africa, this belief takes a Messianic form, coupled with a widespread feeling that in any case they are lost, and it is better to take along as many blacks as possible, with some talk that humanity is better off dead rather than barbarized through rule by black or other colored people. Rumours on research and work on a doomsday machine are spreading.	Counterreasonable (a3)	High intensity (extreme b3)	High risk (c3)	Instrumental, some noninstrumental (d1, some d2)	Counteracceptable (e3)	Crazy martyr country
China	A pure version of Communist ideology is accepted in the leadership, involving commitment to rid the world of capitalism, combined with hostility to white world control. A manifesto calling for united action by all non-whites is published. Widespread famine in China and other Asian countries is blamed on sabotage and weather-control experiments by the United States and Soviet Union. Intense Chinese activities go on in Africa, in South America, and some Asian countries. A strong pro-Chinese party is built up in Japan and strong trade relations are established with Japan, including shared space exploration and space technology. Preparations for an unavoidable clash between China — on behalf of all nonwhite people — and the United States and the Soviet Union serve as a main indoctrination theme. A significant nuclear first-strike capability is being built up, indirectly aided by cooperation with Japan.	Unreasonable (a2)	Medium intensity (b2)	Medium risk (c2)	Instrumental, some noninstrumental (d1, some d2)	Accepted, some accepted ritualistic (e1, some e1a)	Somewhat crazy country
Mexico	Increasing incidents with Mexican-Americans in the United States cause public furor in Mexico and pressures for the Mexican government to provide protection to Mexicans in the United States. Various self-defense activities are promoted in the United States, including counterterror. Relations with Cuba and anti-American revolutionary regimes in a growing number of South American states are strengthened. Demands for return to Mexico of former Mexican territories occupied by the United States get popular support. United States protests are branded as gunboat diplomacy. Defense budget is tripled and a large number of laboratories for esoteric weapons largely staffed by life scientists is established, together with an accelerated nuclear program.	Unreasonable to counterreasonable (a2 to a3)	Medium intensity to high intensity (b2 to b3)	Medium risk (c2)	Instrumental, some noninstrumental (d1, some d2)	Accepted, some unaccepted (e1, some e2)	Somewhat crazy country

Table 3-1, cont.

					Resulting States of Craziness		
Present States	Transformation Phases	Goal Contents	Goal Commitment	Risk Propensity	Means-Goals Relation	Style	Crazy State Prototype Approximated
Indonesia	A charismatic leader supported by the army takes over. He renews expansionistic demands, modernizes the army, builds up a strong party machinery, and accelerates nuclear programs. Terrorist infiltration into neighbouring countries, supported by local groups, takes place. Strong support is received from the Soviet Union, which hopes to build up Indonesia as a potential anti-Chinese aggressive force. With growing vigor, Indonesia pursues a policy of hegemony in the East Indies and presents demands for Australia to become an open settlement area for Asian immigrants, and ultimately an Asian nation.	Unreasonable to counterreasonable (a2 to a3)	Medium intensity to high intensity (b2 to b3)	Medium risk (c2)	Instrumental, some noninstrumental (d1, some d2)	Accepted, some accepted ritualistic (e1, some e1a)	Somewhat crazy country
Kuwait	An extreme religious group takes over control of Kuwait and tries to make it into the center of new vigorous pan-Islam movement, patterned on a puritanistic version. The need to cleanse the world by fire and sword stands in the center of the new sect. Important decisions are made by a small group which uses drugs to achieve ecstasy and states of trance. Careful pressures on oil companies constantly increase the income of Kuwait, all of which is devoted to building up the new movement, with great investments in a small but highly equipped army. Experts in nuclear technology and missile technology from all over the world are hired, and large laboratory and production facilities are built up, with high bribes being offered for scarce knowledge and secret equipment.	Counterreasonable (a3)	High intensity (b3)	High risk (c3)	Noninstrumental to Counteraccepted counterinstrumental (d2 to d3)	Counteraccepted (b3)	Crazy noninstrumental martyr country
Ghana	Through coup d'etat, an aggressive group gains control of the country. A pan-African policy is adopted, taking the form of a Greater African Coprosperity Sphere to be led by Ghana. Unification of black Africa is the goal. Demands for great sums of reparations for years of misuse to be paid by the European countries, the United States, and India are put forth. A network of underground parties covering the whole of black Africa is built up, with the central facilities in some Central African republics supporting the Greater Africa policy.	Unreasonable (a2)	Medium intensity (b2)	Medium risk (c2)	Instrumental, some noninstrumental (d1, some d2)	Unaccepted (b2)	Somewhat crazy country
Czechoslovakia	Some liberalization signs in the Soviet Union are mistaken as a license for more independence. Liberal leaders gain the upper hand and relax political and economic controls. When Soviet counterpressures are activated, rumours begin to circulate that Czechoslovakia has some nuclear warheads, produced with the help of "friends in other countries." The leaders speak darkly about liberty or death, suicide squadrons are organized among students and workers, weapons are distributed to the population – including geiger counters and a leaflet on how to survive a nuclear attack.	Counterreasonable from the point of view of the Soviet Union (a3) Unreasonable from point of view of United States (ab2)	High intensity (b3)	High risk (c3)	Instrumental, some noninstrumental (d1, some d2)	Unaccepted (b2)	Somewhat crazy martyr country

		Reasonable to unreasonable	Medium intensity	Medium risk	Instrumental, some noninstrumental	Accepted	Slightly crazy tendency
France	Increasing internal turmoil and cleavages in the Gaullist party combine to result in widespread disturbances, leading to a general strike and widespread terror. A group composed of generals and senior civil servants takes over the government, with the help of the armed forces. The takeover is greeted with a feeling of relief by most of the population. Public order is restored through use of force. An aggressive foreign policy is followed, directed at breaking up the Common Market unless it fully accepts French hegemony. There is talk that in fact France protects Europe against both the Russians and the United States, and therefore other European countries should accept French hegemony. Pressure is put on Belgium to have the French-speaking part establish a special relationship with France, and on Western Germany to revise the Ruhr situation and have it join France. The nuclear program is accelerated, with emphasis on a large fleet of nuclear submarines with medium-range missiles. In other European countries, there is talk that because of United States neoisolationism, the only hope for security is a United Europe, led by France.	(a1 to a2)	(b2)	(c2)	(d1, some d2)	(b1)	
Extreme Black Group in the United States	An extreme group of blacks organizes an underground demanding establishment of an independent black state in parts of the former United States. Widespread terror is directed at both blacks and whites, with preference on counterpopulation terror tactics; aircrafts, transportation, recreation areas, schools, etc.	Counterreasonable (a3)	High intensity (extreme b3)	High risk (c3)	Noninstrumental (d2)	Counteraccepted (b3)	Crazy martyr noncountry unit
Extreme student groups	An extreme group of former students in various Western countries adopts an anarchistic ideology and initiates action to break up present society. There is indiscriminate counterpopulation terror, with sporadic assassination of local and national politicians and senior executives. There is talk about radioactive terror to be used by this group, which has among its members some brilliant graduate students of physics.	Counterreasonable (a3)	High intensity (extreme b3)	High risk (c3)	Noninstrumental (d2)	Counteraccepted (b3)	Crazy martyr noncountry unit
Extreme Palestinian Refugee Group	A settlement of the Middle Eastern conflict agreed upon by Egypt, Jordan, and Israel is rejected by an extreme Palestinian refugee group. This group is provided with shelter in Syria. It engages in terror against Arab leaders, from time to time blowing up aircraft and trains. Its membership includes a number of professionals and intellectuals and it receives support from China.	Counterreasonable (a3)	High intensity (extreme b3)	High risk (c3)	Noninstrumental (d2)	Counteraccepted (b3)	Crazy martyr noncountry unit
International Scientists for Peace	An international secret club of scientists, especially physicists and chemists, reaches the conclusion that only complete disarmament can prevent destruction of human race. They decide to commit themselves to forcing the major countries to disarm. A manifesto is published, announcing existence of the club and calling on all people of good will to support its goals. The manifesto speaks about the necessity to use force to prevent outdated politicians in all countries from ruining humanity.	Unreasonable to counterreasonable (a2 to a3)	Medium intensity to high intensity (b2 to b3)	High risk (c3)	Instrumental (d1)	Counteraccepted (b3)	Crazy martyr noncountry unit

Note: These scenarios are selected in no particular order from a much larger group of candidates. They are intended purely as hypothetical illustrations, without any implication that the selected countries are necessarily more prone to craziness than others. The concepts are used as explained in Chapter 2.

The scenarios are open to criticism as absurd. Everyone making such a critique is invited to write a scenario based on the situation in Germany in 1920 and predicting Nazism. Every such scenario would surely be judged in 1920 not only as absurd, but as totally impossible and completely crazy. Therefore, despite their oversimplicity and their low probability, some developments in the direction of craziness on lines similar to one or another of the here-presented scenarios should be regarded as possible and, in the aggregate, even as significantly probable.

To enrich the perspective and illustrate possible emergence of crazy states, I outline a variety of transformations in Table 3-1. Detailed construction of scenarios for all the possibilities outlined in Table 3-1 (and additional ones) would be an elegant exercise—and an unnecessary one for this book. Such an exercise might also be more misleading than helpful, because it could create the impression that it is possible to predict (a) the emergence of a crazy state; and (b) the objective probability that such an occurrence would take place under specific conditions and in identified countries. This is misleading because contemporary knowledge is insufficient to support any specific or even stochastic predictions in respect to concrete situations (though some early indicators of propensity toward craziness may be identifiable).

One type of generalized findings which can be derived from the set of scenarios and from the little known on social macrochange deals with factors increasing the probability of radicalized social change, including the possibility of crazy states. Factors which increase possibilities for radical change, including the emergence of craziness as one result—though not necessarily the most probable one—seem to include the following items.

1. Widespread disillusion with contemporary values and search for a new faith to live by. This situation seems to be getting stronger in the saturated countries in which classical religion has lost influence and in which search for material goods is of decreased significance.
2. Strong frustrations caused by inability to achieve minimum levels of aspiration. This is the case in many of the so-called development countries, where aspirants are constantly raising their sights.
3. Intense feelings of deprivation, repression, and injustice caused by easily identifiable and visible enemies. This is the case, for instance, with some members of the black community in the United States. This may also become the case in relations between different races, for instance, antiwhite movements in Africa, and perhaps even new global antiwhite movements by other races.
4. Availability of mass mind-control and mass suggestion devices, whether chemical, communicative, or psychological. This is not an immediate situation, but one which can be expected not very distant in the future.

Each of these four variables seems to be on the increase; therefore, my conclusion is that the probability of crazy states is increasing (though this does not mean that there is a danger of a high probability). The trend is, I think, in the direction of a higher probability of crazy states occurring in the world, though no specific probability distribution can be presented.

This conclusion assumes that all other relevant variables are unchanged, including, in particular, absence of countercraziness measures. Here, we get into one of the paradoxes of all policy-oriented research: if this book succeeds in its mission by encouraging attention to the possibility of crazy states and leading ultimately to some countercraziness measures, and if in the foreseeable future no crazy states appear, then it is impossible to say whether my prediction is right and crazy states would have appeared but for the countermeasures, or whether crazy states would not have occurred and all countermeasures were a waste of resources. It is even possible that if some crazy states do appear, the very measures designed to prevent crazy states may be blamed for actually causing crazy states to happen, by breaking taboos and putting ideas into the wrong heads. This is a problem shared by all policy studies including strategic studies (applying, for instance, also to the issue of deterrence). But it should be recognized explicitly. Especially, the hopefully negative correlation between the probability of crazy states and countercrazy state-oriented strategies deserve careful attention.

The finding that crazy states are a possibility does not by itself make crazy states a significant strategic problem. In order to become a significant strategic problem, crazy states must possess external-action capabilities. When a super-country or a major country becomes crazy, it has the external-action capabilities to translate its craziness into global behavior. But if the significance of craziness is limited to supercountries and major countries, the problem is a limited one. The number of such countries is small; there are no indicators that supercoun-tries and major countries are more susceptible to craziness than are other countries; and, in any case, many may think that there is not much that can be done in advance to deal with the low probability of a supercountry or a major country going crazy. I do not agree with the last statement, because I think there is a lot that can be done to counteract possible transformation into craziness—even in major countries. But I do agree that for crazy states to be a significant problem for strategic studies, the probability of craziness in the supercountries and in the major countries may be insufficient. In order to gain a correct image of the problem of crazy states, the question is, Do the medium, minor, and microcountries and the nonstate units which may become crazy constitute significant strategic problems? Therefore, it is necessary to examine the capacity of such crazy states to develop external-action capabilities which make craziness a significant strategic issue.

4

External-Action Capabilities of Crazy States

I am using the term external-action capabilities to refer to the resources and instruments available to a multiactor for external use, instead of the too broad and unclear term, power, or the too narrow concept, war potential.

The subject of external-action capabilities of countries (and other units) is surrounded by many mistaken notions, all of them tending to underrate the potential capabilities of various states, and of minor and microcountries and noncountry units in particular. Influenced by usual historic patterns on the one hand and by the convex mirror effect on the other, United States strategic studies tend usually to downgrade the external-action capabilities of other countries. Long-standing preoccupation with bipolar models of the international scenery further reinforces the tendency to underrate the potential external-action capabilities of other international multiactors.

Widespread images of the weakness of less-than-major countries and the inability of minor countries and microcountries to develop significant external-action capabilities may be justified in respect to normal situations. But when we are looking for extraordinary events which break routine and reshape strategic situations, expectations with respect to the external-action capabilities of countries and other units must be revised.

The concept of external-action capabilities is a difficult one theoretically.[1] It is a difficult one because it presumes to aggregate in one concept quite a number of heterogeneous capabilities. External-action capabilities include a range of action instruments which have different degrees of effectiveness with respect to various goals and under a variety of circumstances. Therefore, instead of speaking about external-action capabilities, more specific consideration of detailed action capacity is required. At the very least, the concept of external-action capabilities should be perceived as a multidimensional vector, the operation of which depends on the characteristics of the field within which the vector is activated. What is needed—among other requirements—is a fusion of (a) the abstract concept of external-action capabilities; and (b) a geopolitical analysis of particular circumstances (with both variables changing dynamically with variations in relevant conditions, including technology, politics, culture, economy, etc.). When we also take into consideration that because of the illusions of distance,[2] classical concepts of geopolitics are outdated, with major countries having a nearly universal potential presence and even minor countries being able sometimes to operate from far away—then the inadequacies of any simple concept of external-action capability become obvious.

As a result of those complexities, a choice must be made between detailed consideration of concrete situations or a generalized treatment of prototypes. This is a difficult choice when the problems of external-action capabilities are the focus of consideration and analysis. But for our purposes, the preferable solution is clear: since I am operating with prototypes of crazy states, I can regard external-action capabilities as one of the features of those prototypes. Therefore, a generalized treatment of external-action capabilities does not endanger relevance of the crazy state prototypes for reality, because, in any case, no identity with any concrete present situations is claimed. All that I am doing is to establish some prototypes which with the help of reality can be analyzed. This same method, used in Chapter 2 with respect to the concept of crazy states, can also be used, in principle, with respect to external-action capabilities. A number of dimensions of external-action capabilities will accordingly be identified and a number of prototypes of external action will be constructed, with main attention to more extreme situations.

The basic features of external-action capabilities can be analyzed in terms of a three-factor model: one factor includes the external-action capabilities infrastructure, with variables such as size, population, GNP, manpower, research and development, culture, politics, values, and basic social institutions. The second factor includes transformation variables determining the external-action capability realization capacities, including motivation, political capacity, and administrative capacity. The third factor includes the dimensions of external-action capabilities, themselves, including: communication instruments; decision and command and control, military instruments; and vulnerability. The infrastructure provides the maximum production function of external-action capabilities; the realization variables transform the infrastructure variables into external-action capabilities; and the dimensions of external-action capabilities provide a breakdown into external-action instruments. The operation of this model can be seen in the following mode. The external-action capability infrastructure is processed by the realization variables and produces the various dimensions of external-action capabilities (see Table 4-1).

The interaction between the different factors and the intense interrelations must be recognized. Thus, infrastructure variables are, themselves, dependent, in the longer run, on some of the transformation variables, such as motivation and political capability. Even more so, the realization variables are dependent on, and to some extent, even a function of, the infrastructure variables. Nevertheless, for clarification and breakdown of the issue into analyzable components, the simplified model is sufficient.

Table 4–1
Simplified Model of Variables that Shape External Action Capability

External-Action Capability Infrastructure		External-Action Capability Realization Variables		Dimensions of External-Action Capability

Size
Population
GNP
Manpower
R & D
Culture
Various other social
  institutions
	X	Motivation
		Political capacity
		Administrative capacity
			=	Communication
				Economic
				Decision, command
				  and control
				Military: Conventional
				  Nuclear
				  Infra-
				    conventional
				  Ultra-
				    conventional
				Vulnerability

The same model applies also to noncountry units, with suitable adjustments—particularly in respect to the dependence of such units on their environment, which is more intense than the dependence of countries on their environment, even though, in many respects, this is more of a quantitative than of a qualitative difference.

Available literature on external-action capabilities tends to a narrow view of the transformability of the infrastructure into external-action capabilities. The infrastructure does pose absolute limits, at least in the short range, on external-action capabilities. But those limits are much broader than is usually assumed in strategic studies. True, a country cannot have more soldiers than its total adult and teenage population (plus possible import of manpower). But by a suitable system of active reserves, actual armed forces strength can approximate most of the adult population of a country—as illustrated, for instance, by Sweden and even more so by Israel. There are no absolute barriers to devotion of much larger percentages of GNP to building up external-action capacities. As we shall see, nuclear weapons provide an ever greater possibility for relatively small countries to build external-action capabilities which seem completely disproportional to their infrastructure.

Actual external-action capabilities can be much larger in proportion to the infrastructure than is usually the case and is usually supposed to be possible.[a] But it is also possible for a country to have a very large infrastructure without transforming it into actual external-action capabilities. This possibility is illustrated, for instance, by the present situation in Japan, where a rapidly growing infrastructure is not accompanied as yet by any building up of parallel actual external-action capabilities, because of the characteristics of the transformation variables. Most West European countries have a similar tendency. Because of the importance of the transformation variables, efforts to influence them constitute a main aim of adversaries. Internal political and cultural factors fulfill a main role in shaping the extent of transformation of infrastructure into external-action capabilities. Thus, pacifistic tendencies can result in increasing the gulf between growing infrastructures and external-action capabilities.

In order to build prototypes of possible crazy states, my artificial assumption, at least initially, is that the transformation variables operate perfectly. In other words—the full potential of the external-action capability infrastructure is realized. In fact, this is impossible, though one of the characteristics of a crazy instrumental state may be significant efforts to realize a maximum of external-action capability within the limits of the infrastructure (which, itself, will also be subjected to improvement,[b] together with efforts to import external-action capabilities, which I will discuss soon). Nevertheless, a significant degree of realization of the potential (determined by the infrastructure) is possible, more so in smaller countries than in larger ones because they are more manageable. This is an advantage of minor countries and microcountries, which can realize a larger percentage of their potential than larger countries, if they have a high-quality administrative and political system.

Concerning noninstrumental crazy states, the situation is different: a significant amount of instrumental rationality is required to realize large percentages of external-action capability potentials. The question whether it is possible to combine noninstrumentality (with respect to some goals-means relations) with instrumentality (with respect to other means-goals relations) is an

---

[a]An interesting illustration involves transformation of the majority of the population into components of a civil defense system. This can be done, for instance, by (a) getting most of the population to participate in shelter building during a nuclear crisis; or (b) activating the population in a massive nonviolent defense system. The strategic uses of nonviolent defense systems raise interest possibilities. But they are not designed for aggressive action and therefore, they do not constitute a suitable action instrument for crazy states. Also, nonviolent defense systems rely ultimately on the unwillingness of the adversary to use extreme violence; therefore, they are ineffective against a crazy state. Since they are irrelevant for my subject, I will not deal with them further in this book.[3]

[b]The case of Nazi Germany is illuminating in this context because it shows the difficulties of maintaining islands of instrumental-rationality within a crazy state. Especially striking was the inability to approximate total conversion of infrastructure into external-action capabilities, despite the ideological commitment to do so.[4]

open one. Nevertheless, by definition, a noninstrumental crazy state must be inhibited by its instrumental-irrationality in transforming its infrastructure into external-action capability. But this may not prevent islands of instrumentality within the seas of noninstrumentality. Thus, for instance, significant nuclear activities may be engaged in with some isolation of those activities from broad irrational movements and decision patterns. Recent cases do provide indicators that this is possible, at least for a limited time—which may be sufficient to permit a crazy state, which, in many facets of its behavior, is noninstrumental, nevertheless, to build up an instrumental-rationality-based capability in respect to significant military instruments.

In considering the maximum external-action capabilities that can be developed by a crazy state, the following points must be considered.

1. The relationship between usual classifications of countries and their external-action capabilities is an interesting one. Countries can be classified with the help of different criteria, such as: population, manpower with different qualifications, GNP, size, agricultural land, population density and population dispersal, investment in R&D, and many more. More difficult is the use of criteria which are very important but much less tangible, such as: administrative capacities, political cohesion, policy-making qualities, "national culture," etc. No positive correlation between these different criteria within countries exists; therefore, ordering of countries depends on the weight allocated to different criteria and no universal ordering of countries which would be equally useful for all purposes is possible.[5]

Nevertheless, for a general overview, countries can be divided roughly into five categories:

(a) *Super countries*: U.S.A. and U.S.S.R. (complete contents of this category)

(b) *Major countries*: China, England, France, Japan, and others

(c) *Medium countries*: Argentina, Italy, Sweden, and others

(d) *Minor countries*: Israel, New Zealand, Norway, and others

(e) *Microcountries*: Hong Kong, Kuwait, Trinidad-Tobago, and others.

For our purposes, it does not really matter whether we categorize India, for instance, as a major or medium country. In my analysis, I will classify different types of crazy states according to their external-action capabilities, without referring to the infrastructure—which is closely correlated with the general classification of countries. But it is important to keep in mind that external-action capabilities are dependent of more basic variables, which are a part of the infrastructure, and can change quite rapidly within the limits of the infrastructure (plus import possibilities).

2. Though unsolved, the problems of classification of countries and estimation of their external-action capabilities have received considerable attention and have been somewhat clarified in strategic studies. But the classification and estimation of the external-action capabilities of noncountry units are completely *terra incognita*. This is a subject which urgently needs intense attention, because of the growing importance of noncountry units as multiactors of broad—including strategic—significance. For the limited purposes of this study, a pragmatic classification by available external-action capabilities will serve. But this is no substitute for necessary research which will permit more systematic treatment of this issue.

3. There exist about 100 microcountries, including some with rich resources. It is therefore important to emphasize the possibility of some microcountries developing a significant external-action capability, a development which may go hand-in-hand with transformation into a crazy state. The existence of a large number of microstates, most of whom lack any resources, increases the danger that one of them may become a crazy state and develop external-action capabilities of at least regional significance, without any early attention being paid to this occurrence while simple countermeasures may still be effective. This danger increases (though, in absolute terms, its probability may still remain low) when we take into account the possibility that advancing technology may supply external-action instruments which would permit even microstates to achieve very powerful weapon systems, especially nuclear and ultraconventional ones.[c]

4. The importance of communication instruments as a significant dimension of external-action capabilities should not be underrated. Insofar as a crazy state has an ideology which can be exported, that is, which has potential appeal to others, communication of the ideology to audiences in other countries (or in the same country, when what we talk about is a noncountry crazy group) represents an important strategy. Building a significant external-action capability with respect to communication instruments is not difficult: the financial resources and professional manpower requirements for building excellent radio programs directed abroad are limited. Even most of the microcountries—and certainly all minor countries—can build such a capability

---

[c]This applies in part, even more so to noncountry units. It is interesting to speculate on the possibility that new technologies may supply very small units with very powerful weapons. This may result in far-reaching changes in the structure of government, such as splintering up of nonintegrated countries into independent small units, each one of which possesses powerful weapons. The development of local warlords with crude nuclear bombs is a distinct possibility in parts of Africa, Asia and South America. This possibility poses novel strategic issues which are ignored in contemporary strategic studies. The crazy-state issue is only one such issue—although an especially serious one.

if they want to. Television is more expensive and printed material requires distribution networks, but they are relatively unrestrained by a small infrastructure. Noncountry units which cannot build up their own communication instruments may use some other strategy (e.g., blackmail) to gain access to communication instruments of other multiactors; or they can use the characteristics of contemporary mass media to get coverage with little cost or risk to themselves. But one should bear in mind that conversion does not succeed through the use of only written material or broadcasts alone. Building up the necessary network of preachers, agitators, agents, etc.—this requires significant investments.

5. Economic instruments raise interesting issues, commonly neglected in modern strategic studies. I am using the term economic in the broader sense of the term, including various subdimensions such as trade relations, economic aid in the form of grants and loans, technical assistance by supply of manpower, currency manipulations, special trade agreements, export and import controls, and so on.[d] Capacities to develop these instruments depend significantly on infrastructure: a country which has no professional manpower will have great difficulty sending trained technicians abroad. But here, again, more can be done than is usually assumed. Even minor countries can develop significant economic external-action instruments by putting their minds to the matter and looking for specific advantages or trying to develop them. Control over strategic raw materials is a well-recognized case. Another is careful nourishment of forms of technical assistance which, while small in dimensions, achieve a significant impact (because of specialization in critical functions).

6. External-action capabilities can be built up beyond the limitations of the infrastructure with the help of imports. Therefore, import of external-action instruments is an important preferable strategy for crazy states (but, of course, not only for them).

Imports of external-action instruments can take a variety of shapes, including the following specifics.

(a) Open trade relations, such as buying of weapons or hiring of experts, when an open market or a quasiopen market exists.[6]

(b) Limited market buying, when information, manpower, and goods which are restricted can be received through special arrangements with the supplier, either on a commercial basis or on a political basis—with or without payment in goods, in political goodwill, in bases, etc.

---

[d]The Nazis were experts in the utilization of such means, especially in the Balkan countries. The Nazi case also shows that different external-action instruments must be used in combinations. They used economic instruments with communication instruments with (in the final stages) military force.

(c) Black-market buying, to get information, personnel, and equipment—either by paying directly for it or through espionage, kidnapping, stealing, etc.

(d) Systematic absorption of the external-action capabilities of other multiactors and their infrastructure, through conquest, alliances, selective occupation, etc.

As will be shown later in respect to specific military instruments, possibilities for importing external-action instruments are very plentiful. A country or unit endowed with financial resources usually has little difficulty getting what it wants, if necessary through the black market. More difficult is the situation for countries which do not have adequate financial resources to penetrate into the black market of external-action instruments. Also, in respect to some particular items of information or large weapon systems, no available supplier may exist. For many crazy states, the absence of financial and other resources would be a real barrier, but for the availability of some suppliers who take payment in political goodwill (and sometimes take no identifiable payment whatsoever). The availability of opportunities to import external-action instruments is a critical issue. On the one hand, a preferable strategy for crazy states is to maximize import of external-action instruments; on the other hand, a preferable countercraziness strategy is to minimize import of external-action capabilities into crazy states. But, in principle, the availability of instruments which can be imported and which can overcome, to some degree, the limitations of endogenous infrastructure, is important.

7. Vulnerability must be taken into account. In the narrow sense of the term, vulnerability to action by others is not a part of external-action instruments. But when we consider external-action capabilities of other multiactors (particularly those with which the crazy state may come into conflict) vulnerability does constitute a main factor in evaluating the external-action capabilities of the crazy state, itself. Therefore, vulnerability—of the crazy state as a whole and of its external-action instruments in particular—does constitute one of the basic dimensions of external-action capability.

8. Passing on to a more detailed consideration of military external instruments, it is necessary to distinguish between four subdimensions: (a) conventional military instruments; (b) nuclear (often called unconventional) military instruments; (c) infraconventional military instruments (insurgence, subvergence, sabotage, etc.); and (d) ultraconventional military instruments (biochemical and radioactive weapons, and similar more intense than conventional instruments, but not nuclear explosives).

There is considerable overlap among the weapons in these four subdimensions, e.g., nuclear tactical weapons, nuclear barriers, radioactive poisoning without nuclear explosions, paraphysical weapons (e.g., operating through noise), chemical weapons used for sabotage, and biological doomsday machines. Though this classification system has limited validity, let me use it as a basic skeleton for a consideration of military external-action instruments.

Conventional Military External-Action Instruments

Conventional military external-action instruments are not unique to crazy states and are better understood in strategic studies than other types of military external-action instruments. Therefore, for the purposes of this book, it is less necessary to go into many details.

I have already pointed out some of the fallacies concerning belief in the rigidity of infrastructure constraints on conventional military capabilities and I have mentioned the possibility of transforming a larger part of infrastructure into conventional military instruments. There are a number of additional points which should be made.

1. It is easier to import conventional military instruments than it is to import other types of military instruments. But these imports are usually standard types which may not fit local requirements and conditions. Therefore, maximization of external-action capabilities in many crazy states (and also in most of the normal states) requires development of specific doctrines, organizational structures, and equipment to fit the needs of the countries within their specific geopolitics situation. This does not imply that imports cannot be useful; but shopping must be selective and conversion techniques to adjust hardware to local needs must be available. Particularly critical is the capacity to develop suitable doctrines which are related to specific policies and contingencies of the crazy state.

2. Within the domain of conventional military instruments, innovative systems must be developed to meet the need of crazy states—a requirement which cannot be met by a crazy state with ritualistic stylistic fixations. To illustrate: some of the problems facing a crazy state with respect to its conventional military instruments are: (1) the relative roles of Air Force, Navy, and Land Forces; (2) the functions of special forces; (3) trade-offs between fire power and mobility; (4) trade-offs between smaller cadres of professional troops or a citizen army; (5) preferable combinations of conventional, nuclear, infraconventional, and ultraconventional instruments; and (6) the advantages of ready forces versus mobilizable forces. These and similar problems are shared by

normal and crazy states, but the solutions will differ for crazy states—as will be indicated when I reach the preferable strategies for crazy states. But already here some considerations specific to crazy states can be indicated.

Because of the dependence of preferable solutions on specific conditions and missions, elaboration of military doctrines, structures, and equipment is impossible in the abstract. But to illustrate the opportunities for crazy states to gear themselves for significant external activities with the help of conventional military instruments, let me mention the following items.

(a) Specialized units for occupying political control and command centers of an adversary (especially if the adversaries are underdeveloped countries which cannot be expected to have strong defenses of their political centers). Helicopters can provide striking capabilities for surprise attack on political centers.
(b) Fast penetration (with small units without extensive logistic capabilities) to overrun an adversary before he can mobilize.
(c) Preemptive counterforce air strikes, which can completely annihilate the military instruments of an adversary.

Such illustrations are dangerously misleading because they ignore defensive contingency plans. They are, therefore, only intended to show how crazy states could use suitably conventional military instruments in effective ways.

Nuclear Military External-Action Instruments

There are few subjects in the United States strategic studies and strategic policies that are as mixed up as the subject of nuclear weapon development in other countries. Because of the convex mirror effect (discussed in Chapter 1), there is a strong tendency in American strategic studies to regard nuclear weapons as bad for other countries, inter alia, because those countries are unable to develop stable nuclear weapon systems with second-strike capacity, protected command and control, and graduated strike ability. In the next chapter, we will deal with the possibility of crazy states using nuclear weapons for preferable strategies. At present, we are only looking into the feasibility of developing nuclear weapons capabilities in crazy states. In respect to this issue, there is clearly a great difference between a major country and microcountry. A major crazy country can develop a well-rounded, though limited, nuclear capability if it is willing to pay the price (which it may be, if nuclear weapons are preferable instruments for its goals). When we take medium, minor, and microcountries, possibilities are more limited. Nevertheless, possibilities to develop nuclear instruments exist for medium, minor and even microcountries. Such capabilities will be qualitatively different from the nuclear capabilities of the United States and the Soviet Union. But they are not designed to meet the same needs and may fit their specific conditions as well as the American nuclear weapon systems meet their strategic purposes. In considering the feasibility of development of nuclear weapons for crazy states, the following considerations must be taken into account.[7]

1. Thanks to the increased use of nuclear reactors for peaceful purposes, the difficulties of developing a small number of low-yield fission bombs are greatly reduced. The knowledge required for doing so is available. Enriched uranium is not very difficult to get, especially if the interested crazy state makes a suitable initial investment in nuclear reactors for peaceful purposes, such as energy production. The Non-Proliferation Treaty may provide more help than hindrance in preparation for nuclear weapons production, thanks to the inspection system which gives crazy states convenient learning opportunities.[8] Also, by signing the Non-Proliferation Treaty, a state can claim aid in peaceful uses of nuclear energy and open ways for later conversion to military uses.

2. A crazy state may develop a limited number of nuclear bombs either secretly or more or less openly. Even if it did sign the Non-Proliferation Treaty, realistic inspections may not inhibit diversion of material for military uses. Also, withdrawal from the Non-Proliferation Treaty after one has built up a peaceful nuclear capability is a possible road to a limited first-strike capability.

3. Technological innovations may make it possible to produce advanced nuclear bombs, such as fusion bombs. Widespread use of reactors which use enriched uranium, development of centrifugal separation techniques, and other predicted innovations may provide opportunities for countries with limited nuclear programs to produce small numbers of high-yield nuclear weapons.

4. Strategic studies in the United States tend to downgrade the usefulness of a medium, small, or microcountry having a few nuclear weapons because of (a) the absence of second-strike capability; (b) the absence of delivery capability; and (c) the absence of suitable command and control systems. All these objections may be largely irrelevant. A limited first-strike capability may be all that is needed in order to open up a number of strategies for crazy purposes. Many countries can develop a limited second-strike capability, in the sense of protecting their nuclear capabilities against a possible first strike by their adversary (another medium, minor or microcountry which has itself a very limited first-strike capability). Delivery is no real problem against most

countries. Clandestine delivery, penetration by individual aircraft or rockets, and similar styles of delivery may provide a credible threat and, in some circumstances, may actually be able to deliver nuclear bombs—even against a major country and perhaps even against a supercountry. This may and usually will result in the destruction of the crazy state. Therefore, making a limited threat with a few hidden nuclear bombs against a major of supercountry may be quite incredible, in addition to inviting a first strike. Nevertheless, for some types of crazy states and under some circumstances, such action against a major or even supercountry may be preferable (not only for crazy states), in comparison to all other available alternatives. This, for instance, may be the case if the major or supercountry adopts radical counterstrategies against the crazy state (or normal state) which endanger the latter's very survival.

All the possibilities discussed are feasible and credible in respect to a first counterpopulation strike, which presents sometimes an optimal threat to be made by a crazy state. For threatening and sometimes executing a first counterpopulation strike, command and control is not a real problem. Therefore, difficulty in building up a reliable command and control system which permits graduated response under a variety of contingencies is not really an issue for crazy states.

My conclusion is that crazy states will often be able to develop a limited nuclear capability. Most of them—with the exception of very poor minor and microcountries—are able—or will be able in the foreseeable future—to develop a limited first counterpopulation strike capability. The capability can also constitute a second-strike capability against a medium, minor or microcountry by careful use of hiding, constant movement of the nuclear weapons and some hardening against attack. A second-strike capability against a major or supercountry is much more difficult to achieve. But hiding a limited number of nuclear bombs in other countries or on ships on the high seas may be under some circumstances, a real possibility which should not be ignored. In short, crazy states will be able to develop meaningful nuclear capabilities if they want to do so.

Less clear, and even more disturbing, is the question whether or not noncountry units may be able to gain a limited nuclear capability. Here, the possibilities to be considered include a group stealing or buying nuclear bomb raw materials and making a few primitive nuclear devices to plant and use for blackmail, terror, or efforts to start a war. Some possibilities (mutiny of a nuclear-equipped submarine,[9] a group of scientists developing its own nuclear weapons) seem too esoteric even for the broad framework of this study. Nevertheless, those who regard such possibilities as too science fictionlike to deserve serious consideration should be reminded that science fiction is in a crisis because so many ideas which thirty or forty years ago were considered as pure science fiction have been realized. Therefore, the possibility of noncountry units getting hold of a few primitive nuclear devices is one which should be taken seriously, though it is less probable than the possibility of crazy countries achieving a limited nuclear capability.

Similarly hypothetical is the possibility of a doomsday machine. At present, the most likely form of a doomsday machine is a very dirty (i.e., radioactivity-creating) nuclear device, designed especially to achieve maximum poisoning of the atmosphere. Some experts are of the opinion that such a doomsday machine could be built by any country able and willing to invest significant, but not tremendous resources in it. These experts think that it is only the taboo on the nature of the idea and its obvious uselessness which inhibit work in that direction. Both these inhibitions do not operate with respect to some crazy states; by definition, a counterstylistic crazy state will not be bound by the taboos surrounding a doomsday machine. For a crazy martyr state, a doomsday machine may be an obviously preferable instrument. This possibility is one which must be taken into account (although it has a low probability). Luckily, present technology does not permit construction of doomsday machines by many countries or by noncountry units. But if technology should ever permit easier construction of doomsday machines, a frightening category of crazy state capability must be added to the list of possibilities.[e]

Infraconventional Military
External-Action Instruments

Some types of infraconventional military instruments have received intensive attention during the last ten to twenty years, due to various forms of insurgence, rebellion, and internal wars since World War II. Recently, the subject has been treated within a broader theoretic framework, which overcomes many wide-spread fallacies.[10]

On the subject of infraconventional military instruments for crazy states, a number of points deserve emphasis. These include in particular, the following items.

There are nearly unlimited possibilities for stylistic innovations in respect to infraconventional military instruments. Many of these innovations do not

---

[e]What does one expect a specific multiactor to do if it possesses a doomsday machine? What would one expect a specific multiactor to do if he possessed a total weapon, i.e., a weapon which protected him completely while it permitted him to destroy everyone else selectively? Whether these will remain hypothetical questions and for how long, remains to be seen. I think that even slight approximation of such possibilities (as could occur in the foreseeable future) requires changes in our international system and its control over multiactors.

require a significant infrastructure. They depend on imagination, small groups of devotees, and the attitudes of craziness. Already mentioned are kidnapping of diplomats and their uses for blackmailing, attacks on civil transportation, terror against political leaders, indiscriminate bombings of civilian objectives, terrorizing of selected areas, systematic assassination of leaders and administrators, widespread execution of hostages and destruction of food. These few illustrations should demonstrate the possibilities which do not need complex instruments, and do not require significant infrastructure (and which, as a result are feasible for many crazy states including, in particular, noncountry units). The question is whether or not such instruments are useful with respect to the goals of crazy states. But, in principle, the possibility cannot be doubted. Because of the absence of rigid constraints on such instruments and their easy availability to noncountry units, (who may be prone to such counterstylistic patterns), they are one of the dangers that must be expected.

Ultraconventional Military External-Action Instruments

Under the term ultraconventional military instruments, I include the whole range of potential high-intensity weapons which are neither conventional nor nuclear, even though they can be used in conjunction with conventional nuclear and infraconventional instruments. Illustrations of ultraconventional external-action instruments include biochemical weapons, mind-influencing drugs, weather control used as a weapon, and so on.[11]

With the exception of some weapons such as poison gas, the present state-of-the-art does not supply ultraconventional instruments which are usable. The possibility of a breakthrough, for instance, in biological weapons cannot be ignored; intensive biological research could be fruitful for a crazy state with resources for a high-risk investment. But it is hard to see ultraconventional instruments as main components of the external-action capabilities of crazy states in the foreseeable future. (It is easier to imagine the noncountry units using some such means as mass terror.)

Having explored the dimensions of military external-action instruments, we can now construct some prototypes of external-action capabilities of crazy states. Starting with the classification of states according to infrastructure, as developed in the second chapter, we can make some observations on the maximum external-action capability, dimension by dimension and subdimension by subdimension (see Table 4-2).

Such an elaboration of maximum external-action capabilities provides some surprising insights, particularly with respect to microcountries and minor

Table 4–2
Maximum External-Action Capability of Different States

Type of Capability

Type of State	Communications	Economic	Decision, Command, and Control	Conventional Military	Nuclear Military	Infraconventional Military	Ultraconventional Military	Vulnerability
Supercountry	Saturation capacity through all media	Very strong	Very high quality	Very extensive and comprehensive	All types of first and second strike; also, graduated and elastic uses; Doomsday machine possible now	Very extensive and comprehensive, but hard to camouflage	Extensive R&D and full capabilities in respect to all existing instruments	Of civilian targets – medium; of military targets – low
Major country	Saturation capacity through all media	Strong to very strong	Very high quality	Extensive and comprehensive	Extensive first countervalue strike; some first counter-force strike; some second strike; some graduated and elastic uses; Doomsday machine probably possible now	Extensive and comprehensive, but hard to camouflage	Selective R&D and preparations for capabilities	Of civilian targets – medium; of military targets – low
Medium country	Broadcasting saturation capacity; medium capacity through other media	Medium, sometimes strong in specific areas	Very high quality	Strong all-around capacity, with highly developed; selective capabilities	Medium first countervalue strike; some countervalue second strike; Doomsday machine perhaps possible	Strong regional capabilities, hard to camouflage	Focused R&D and selective capabilities	Of civilian targets – high; of military targets – medium
Minor country	Strong broadcasting capacities; some capacities through other media	Minor, sometimes strong in specific areas	Very high quality	Medium, with highly developed selective capabilities	Some first countervalue strike; minor countervalue second strike; Doomsday machine perhaps possible in future	Strong localized capabilities	Some selective R&D and capabilities	High
Microcountry	Medium to strong broadcasting capacities; some capacities through other media	Very minor, sometimes medium in specific areas	Very high quality	Minor	In the future: Some first countervalue strike; minor countervalue second strike; Doomsday machine perhaps possible	Medium localized capabilities	Some selective R&D and capabilities	High
Noncountry units	Small to medium capacities, mainly localized	None, sometimes some	Very high quality	None	In the future: Some first countervalue clandestine strike; Regional Doomsday machine perhaps possible.	Minor to strong, especially in counterstyled areas	None, with limited exceptions in respect to single instruments	Low to medium

Table 4-3
Levels of External Action Capabilities of Crazy States.

Designation of State	Dimensions of External Action Capabilities							
	Communications	Economic	Decision, Command and Control	Conventional	Nuclear	Infraconventional	Ultraconventional	Vulnerability
Weak state	Low	Low	Low quality	Low	None	None	None	High
Propaganda state	High	Low	Medium	Low	None	None	None	High
Economic influence state	Low	High	Medium	Low	None	None	None	High
Medium conventional forces state	Low to medium	Low to medium	Medium	Medium	None	None	None	Medium
Weak nuclear state	Low to medium	Low to medium	Medium	Low to medium	Some first strike countervalue	None	None	Medium to high
Medium nuclear state	Low to medium	Low to medium	Medium	Low to medium	Medium first strike countervalue; some first strike counterforce and some second strike countervalue	None	None	Population – medium to high; nuclear force – medium, some low
Strong nuclear state	Medium to high	Low to medium	Medium to high	Low to medium	Strong first and second strike, countervalue and elastic special capabilities	None	None	Population – medium; nuclear forces – low
Medium infraconventional state	Medium	Low	Medium	Low or none	None	Medium	None	Low to medium
Strong infraconventional state	Medium to high	Low	High	Low or none	None	High	None	Low
Strong ultraconventional state	Low	Medium	High	Low to medium	None	None	High	Medium
Doomsday state	Medium	Medium	High	Low or none	Doomsday machine (or none)	None	None (or Doomsday machine)	High; of Doomsday machine – low

Note: This table presents 11 qualitative prototypes of External Action Capabilities Levels, as an aid for heuristic analysis. Real states do constitute different mixes of these levels.

Table 4-4
Main Prototypes of Possible Crazy States

Name	Dimensions of Craziness					Dimensions of External-Action Capabilities							
	Goal Content	Goal Commitment	Risk Propensity	Means-Goals Relation	Style	Communications	Economic	Decision, Command, and Control	Conventional	Nuclear	Infraconventional	Ultraconventional	Vulnerability
Crazy propaganda and weak nuclear country	Counter-reasonable	High intensity	Medium risk and some high risk	Instrumental, some noninstrumental	Counter-accepted	High	Low	Medium to high	Low	Some first-strike counter-population	None	None	Medium to high
Crazy medium nuclear country	Counter-reasonable	High intensity	Medium risk and some high risk	Instrumental, some noninstrumental	Counter-accepted	Low	Low	Medium to high	Low	Medium first-strike counter-population; some first-strike counterforce and some second-strike counter-population	None	None	Population – medium to high; nuclear force – medium, some low
Crazy martyr weak nuclear country	Counter-reasonable	High intensity	Extreme high risk	Instrumental, some noninstrumental	Counter-accepted	Low	Low	Medium to high	Low	Some first-strike counter-population	None	None	Medium to high
Crazy noninstrumental martyr weak nuclear country	Counter-reasonable	High intensity	Extreme high risk	Counter-instrumental	Counter-accepted or counter-accepted ritualistic	Low	Low	Low	Low	Some first-strike counter-population	None	None	Medium to high
Crazy medium infraconventional state (country, subcountry or extra-country unit)	Counter-reasonable	High intensity	Medium risk and some high risk	Instrumental, some noninstrumental	Counter-accepted	Low	Low	Medium to high	Low	None	Medium	None	Low
Crazy martyr doomsday state (country or sub-country or extra-country unit)	Counter-reasonable	High intensity	Medium risk and some high risk	Instrumental, some noninstrumental	Counter-accepted	Low	Low	Medium to high	Low	Doomsday machine	None	None	Population – medium or low; Doomsday machine – low
Crazy noninstrumental martyr doomsday state (country or sub-country or extra-country unit)	Counter-reasonable	High intensity	Medium risk and some high risk	Counter-instrumental	Counter-accepted	Low	Low	Low	Low	Doomsday machine	None	None	Population – medium or low; Doomsday machine – low
Crazy medium conventional forces state	Counter-reasonable	High intensity	Medium risk and some high risk	Instrumental, some noninstrumental	Counter-accepted	Low to medium	Low to medium	Medium	Medium	None	None	None	Medium

countries.[f] But, by itself, it is insufficient for analyzing the problem of crazy states because it is too counterfactual to expect crazy states to achieve a maximum development of their external-action capability. To develop a set of realistic prototypes, we must consider capabilities which fall short of maximum hypothetical developments. For this purpose, I identify a number of levels of development which range between zero and maximum development of external-action capability. These levels are presented in Table 4-3 (see p. 56).

It is possible to construct a master list of possible crazy states by cross-tabulating the levels of external-action capabilities with the list of prototypes of craziness, as developed in Table 2-2. This cross-tabulation can provide a set of main combinations which are too large for manageability within the context of this book and too artificial for usefulness. Therefore, I am reducing and processing it into an operational set of possible crazy states, which represent the more detailed list and provide prototypes which permit analysis of the problem. This reduced list is presented in Table 4-4 on p. 57. This list will serve as an initial basis for my analysis in the next chapters. For application to real situations, the prototype analysis must be adjusted to the concrete circumstances of unique cases.

---

[f]The underestimation of the potential external-action capability of small countries is a mistake not limited to United States strategic studies. It is a result of (1) uncritical acceptance of the economies of large scale; and (2) the actual experience of small states which have to make great efforts to achieve a part of what comes naturally to bigger countries.[12]

5 Some Preferable Strategies for Crazy States

The concept of *preferable strategy* is difficult for there is a unique set of goals, conditions, resources, situations, behavior patterns, etc. for each specific situation. But we can identify some main preferable substrategies for possible crazy states. Concrete preferable strategies consist of mixes between substrategies, whose composition is a function of specific circumstances. I will, therefore, (1) examine some preferable substrategies; and (2) explore a number of mixes of these substrategies which could form preferable strategies for crazy states.

Before taking up these substrategies, the following observations are in order.

1. The concept *preferable* refers to a solution which is better than the usual one, but it does not presume to be optimal in the technical sense of that term. Therefore, when speaking about preferable strategies, I refer to strategies which are superior to usual ones (that is, those followed in most cases in practice or discussed most frequently in strategic studies), without claiming that these are the best possible strategies, that is, the optimal ones.

   Identification of optimal strategies requires degrees of sophistication and depth of analyses which are impossible to achieve at the present state of knowledge in strategic theory. This applies in particular to so complex and neglected a subject as crazy states. But it is possible to identify preferable components for strategies to be followed by crazy states, on the level of abstract analysis in respect to crazy state prototypes. These are the preferable substrategies presented in this chapter.

2. By definition, preferable strategies are strategies arrived at through a good strategy-making process, which must be based on "instrumental" relations between goals and means. Therefore, the concept of optimal strategies does not apply to noninstrumental and especially to counterinstrumental crazy states. These states may accidentally hit upon a preferable strategy, and many of their strategies will be composed of the same substrategies as preferable strategies—though in nonpreferable or counterpreferable mixes. Therefore, the components of preferable strategies are less useful for analyzing counterinstrumental crazy states (who cannot be considered as striving for preferable strategies).

59

This point must be emphasized, because it can easily be misunderstood unless the meaning of the term crazy states as used and explained by me in Chapter 1 is kept in mind. As explained, a state can be crazy and instrumental at the same time, the craziness being related to the goal contents, goal commitment, risk propensity and stylistic innovation—but not to the instrumental relation between goals and means.

3. I proceeded from basic characteristics of crazy states to their external-action capabilities and to their preferable strategies. But, it is incorrect to regard strategic choices as completely constrained by the basic characteristics of the involved states and their existing external-action capabilities. External-action capabilities can themselves be significantly shaped through suitable action. Indeed, preferable strategies determine how external-action instruments are developed and the latter are designed to meet the needs of the former. Furthermore, the build-up of a suitable infrastructure is to some extent a subject of important policies. The characteristics of the relevant states can be influenced by encouraging population growth, building up particular branches of the economy and trying to take over certain territories. Thus, changing basic features of the involved state is a subject for action by crazy states. The interdependence of basic features, external-action capabilities, and preferable strategies is close and should be recognized.

4. External actions by crazy states take place within an interaction system.[1] The crazy state is constantly interacting with international multiactors; its preferable strategies depend on the counterstrategies of these multiactors, who shape the counter-counterstrategies of the crazy states, (who determine the counter-counter-counterstrategies of the multiactors and so on). One method for dealing with this interaction problem is in the form of an extended game, i.e., a complete set of moves contingent upon all possible moves of the others. But since we are dealing with an open set of alternatives and a large number of multiactors, an extended form is even theoretically impossible, and the concept is quite useless for applied analysis. Furthermore, it is not only the mutual moves which shape one another; the mutual expectations are powerful determinates of preferable strategies. "I think that you think that I think that you think . . ." this is an important part of a correct image of the processes involved in identifying preferable strategies.

Were we to presume to present detailed strategies for specific situations, the problems of interdependencies between expectations and strategies would have to be handled in detail. But since we are focusing attention on general strategy components, the problem is a less acute one. In the present chapter, the initial preferable strategies of crazy states are our main subject. After considering preferable countercraziness strategies, some of the interaction problems between preferable strategies by crazy states and preferable counterstrategies will become clearer.

5. Preferable strategies are an idealized concept, which will not appear in reality in their pure form. Even approximation is difficult, depending on the existence of a good policy-making system, at least in respect to limited issues. Expected strategies may move somewhat in the direction of preferability if the necessary conditions exist, including high-quality decision-making and command and control capacities as a part of the external-action capabilities. How real strategies will move (in the direction of preferable or counterproductive strategies) depends on the features of crazy states if and when they appear. I have adopted the methodological device of extreme prototypes to clarify basic concepts and bring out underlying issues. With suitable adjustments, the conclusions of the abstract preferable strategy analysis are applicable to real situations.

6. Preferable strategies and their components can operate *vis-a-vis* the target multiactor either directly or indirectly. Directly means the strategies are applied by a crazy state to the adversary without any intervening multiactors. Indirectly, means the crazy state tries to get other multiactors to operate on the adversary to advance its own goals. Efforts to get other multiactors involved constitute a main substrategy of particular importance for crazy minor and microcountries. Quite a number of the substrategies are designed to achieve goals by activating other multiactors who would substitute for the crazy state in conflicts. This is often arranged by provocation, deception, and alliances.

7. The set of preferable strategies for crazy states overlaps, in part, the set of preferable strategies for normal countries. Some strategies which are preferable for normal countries, such as disarmament and bona fide accommodation, do not fit the basic goals of crazy states and are useless for them. Larger is the number of substrategies preferable for crazy states which are useless for normal states, mainly because of their immoral and antimoral characteristics and their high social costs. They are also self-defying since the goals of the normal states include not becoming crazy. This asymmetry raises important issues for the interaction between crazy states and normal states. In the present chapter, I focus mainly on those substrategies and the components which are more unique to crazy states than to normal states.

To clarify some preferable strategies for possible crazy states, I will distinguish between eleven main substrategies, namely: deception; infiltration and take over from within; conversion; erosion; isolation; alliances; provocation; blackmail; occupation; destruction; and—in a somewhat different category—timing. These substrategies should be kept quite distinct from external-action instruments. External-action instruments can serve these different substrategies to various degrees and the existence of suitable instruments is a *sine qua non* for adopting a particular strategy. The relationship between the substrategies and external-action instruments is brought out in Table 5-1.

Table 5-1
External Action Instruments and Preferable Substrategies

Preferable Substrategies	Necessary External Action Instruments							
	Communication	Economic	Decision, Command and Control	Conventional	Nuclear	Infraconventional	Ultraconventional	Vulnerability
Deception	Strong	—	High to very high quality	—	—	—	—	—
Infiltration and take-over from within	Medium to strong	Some	High to very high quality	Some	—	High to very high	—	Medium or low
Conversion	Very strong	Some	High to very high quality	—	—	Some	—	—
Erosion	Medium	Some	High to very high quality	Medium or low	—	Low or medium	—	Medium or low
Isolation	Strong	Some	High to very high quality			Some mix sufficient to constitute a threat	—	—
Alliances	Medium to strong	Low to high	High to very high quality			Some mix sufficient to constitute a threat	—	—
Provocation	Medium to strong	—	Very high quality	Strong	Sometimes: demonstration capabilities	Medium to high	—	Low
Blackmail	Strong	At present: medium in the future: low	Very high quality	Very strong or	First countervalue or First countervalue strike to Doomsday machine	Very strong	Strong to Doomsday machine	Low – at least in respect to blackmail instruments
Occupation	—	Medium to High	Medium to very high quality	High to very high	—	—	—	Medium or low
Destruction	—	At present – medium; in the future: low	Medium to high quality	Very high	or First extensive countervalue and counterforce strike	—	or In the future: high to very high	Low to very low
Timing	—	—	High to very high quality	—	—	—	—	—

Note: The various requirements in this table are stated in relative terms, in respect to the involved target areas. Therefore, calculation of the required absolute quantities of the various instruments depends on the resources, instruments and vulnerability of the target areas. Even so, the table does provide some indication of the importance of different external action instruments for various substrategies.

Table 5-1 also illustrates some of the forms which the preferable substrategies can take, depending on the availability of different external-action instruments. But a number of additional clarifications are necessary in respect to each one of the preferable substrategies in order to examine some of their ramifications.

Deception

Deception is a main substrategy of particular importance for crazy states. A first question is, How should a crazy state try to hide the features of its craziness? (A converse question is, How should a normal state try to present itself as crazy?)[2] As long as a crazy state is expecting possible counteraction by other multiactors to its crazy features, before it is ready to absorb them, efforts to hide craziness are preferable. But, from a certain point, a crazy state may show off its craziness, and take advantage of the unwillingness of the other multiactors to make the investment needed to counter craziness. A subissue is, Should a somewhat crazy state try to make the impression of a more extreme state of craziness, such as a crazy noninstrumental state or a crazy martyr state? In particular, it may be shrewd to create the impression of a martyr crazy state since some accommodation of this type of crazy state is often easier and cheaper than taking more extreme countermeasures.

These are some particular features of the use of deception as a preferable substrategy by crazy states. In general, deception is of broad utility and applies to most of the other substrategies, and to many of the external-action instruments. To illustrate: deception in respect to nuclear instruments presents interesting possibilities, both in building an image that one has more nuclear instruments than one possesses in fact, and in hiding development of nuclear instruments. Deception by camouflaging and hiding nuclear instruments is often a preferable substrategy until there are sufficient nuclear instruments to deter external intervention. From that point—or much earlier if no countercraziness strategies are activated—exaggerating the capability of one's nuclear instruments may be a preferable substrategy, along with blackmail. Similar considerations apply to other external-action instruments, especially military ones. But most problems of deception by crazy states are not unique to them; they are shared with other international multiactors and therefore do not have to be dealt with here in more detail.[3]

Infiltration and Take-Over from Within

Infiltration and take-over from within are recognized substrategies, widely practiced by ideological movements, such as the Nazis and the Communists. The patterns of infiltration and take-over from within include (1) establishment of subversive groups and their support in the target areas; (2) supply of equipment; (3) direct aid, i.e., advisors, camouflaged troops, intelligence, etc.; and (4) guerrilla warfare waged by regular troops of the crazy state. In order to succeed, a number of conditions in the target area must be met, including: (1) propensity to internal disturbance; (2) tendency to support or not to resist active infiltration and take-over; (3) weakness in the governmental and military machinery; and (4) absence of countercraziness interference by strong international multiactors. Insofar as these conditions are realized, infiltration and take-over present a preferable substrategy because they involve relatively low cost and low risks. Even if insufficient by themselves, they can be a valuable element in a broader strategy mix, interacting synergistically with other substrategies.

Conversion

A feature of many of the crazy states is their bona fide commitment to an ideology which they try to propagate and diffuse. Conversion to their ideology is a main goal and a substrategy of the crazy states. It is closely related to infiltration and take-over from within, but emphasizes communication instruments and thus appeals to the emotions and beliefs of the population. Getting the population to adopt the ideology, dogma, and value system of the crazy state by convincing them that these beliefs are the correct ones—this is a primary goal and means of their preferable strategies.

Again, in order to succeed, a number of conditions must be met, including (1) propensity in the target area to adopt a new ideology, dogma, and value system; (2) the crazy state's ideology, dogma and value must be sellable and must appeal to the target population in terms of contents; and (3) suitable development of the external-action instruments needed for conversion, especially communication instruments and networks of converters. Because of the frozen nature of global ideological struggles, the possibility of successful conversion by symbolic external-action instruments and limited support by military instruments does not receive adequate consideration in present strategic studies. But it is possible that large parts of the world may be quite ready for new ideologies, dogmas, and value systems. Therefore, it is possible that a crazy state could make significant impact with a pure conversion substrategy, and confront normal countries with a challenge for which they are completely unprepared. If it can work, conversion is a preferable substrategy.

Erosion

I use the term erosion to refer to what is often called salami tactics, namely, achieving one's goals through phased and incremental take-over of the target area. Examples of this approach include the following items: (1) a preferred trade agreement; (2) a monopoly on military training; (3) a slight border adjustment; (4) a defense alliance in which the crazy state is clearly the dominant partner; (5) a slight interference in the internal domestic political processes of the target area; etc.

The main idea of this substrategy is to operate bit by bit, until a critical mass is achieved which transforms the target area to satisfy the goals of the crazy state. The erosion substrategy cross-cuts the other substrategies and is a way to apply some of them. Thus, occupation, destruction, conversion, infiltration, and take-over—each can proceed at a rapid rate or at a slow erosion rate, with different in-between situations preferable under diverse conditions. One of its main advantages is that it makes it easy to veil one's real purposes and it provokes less reaction than a more radical strategy. Each step can be presented (and accepted by adversaries) as a last and final demand, one to be accepted rather than take countermeasures. Nazi Germany provides many illustrations of successful use of the erosion substrategy. As long as an erosion substrategy prevents countercraziness action, it is a preferable strategy.

Isolation

Because of the interconnectedness of the world, isolating an adversary is essential. Judicious use of a number of incentives, both positive and negative, directed at the adversary and the multiactors who are supporting him, is necessary in order to achieve some degree of isolation. Often, deception concerning the real goals of the crazy state is needed to isolate its adversary from external support. Direct pressure on the adversary with other substrategies to force him to detach himself from his allies illustrates the interdependence of substrategies.

Alliances

Manipulation of alliances is a main substrategy related to involving other multiactors to operate on behalf of the interests and goals of the crazy state. As discussed in Chapter 4, it is also a main substrategy to build external-action capabilities. The capacity of countries to improve their positions with suitable alliance strategies is quite surprising, but clearly illustrated by history. A crazy state will prefer alliances with other crazy states with similar or compatible ideologies, goals, and other dimensions of craziness. Alliances with normal countries are also possible and desirable under some circumstances, though their feasibility may depend on successful deception. The purpose of alliance strategy for a crazy state, in addition to try to gain active support for its activities, is to inhibit countercraziness strategies and to isolate the adversary. Also, through alliances, international multiactors can be hindered in recognizing the true nature of the crazy state and can be diverted from taking necessary countercraziness measures. Furthermore, countries not allied with the crazy state can be deterred by the alliances, and they may regard the alliance as an indicator of normal behavior.

The possibilities for action of crazy states can be improved by playing the alliance substrategy well. The dependence of successful countercraziness strategies on countercrazy alliances increases even more the importance of this substrategy. Under contemporary conditions, playing the United States vs. the Soviet Union with suitable relations with the "third world," China, France, and other main international multiactors—can provide an especially fruitful field for an imaginative and initiative-full alliance substrategy by crazy states.

Provocation

Provocations are actions designed to get some other international multiactors to engage in overreactive behavior which somehow is in the interest of the provoker. A form of provocation involves initiation of negative interaction between a number of multiactors by anonymous provocation or provocation which looks as if it originates with one of them. The list of possible anonymous or misrepresented triggering provocative actions is very large, ranging from single dramatic acts of terror made to look as if committed by someone else to anonymous explosion of nuclear devices. Insofar as provocation can weaken potential adversaries or isolate them from their potential supporters, it is a highly preferable strategy (if the risks of detection and radical counteraction can be discounted). Risks of detection is always significant; therefore, provocation by anonymous or misrepresented activities is an undesirable substrategy for low-risk actors. But crazy states with a high-risk propensity may regard anonymous provocation as a preferable substrategy—particularly when other substrategies fail or are unavailable. The most extreme illustration is the triggering of a catalytic nuclear war between supercountries by anonymous or misrepresented nuclear explosions. Assuming the supercountries remain more or less normal, this is an operation with very low probability of success. But less ambitious efforts at initiation of local wars and breaking of alliances and mutual support arrangements by anonymous provocation do present an opportunity. This substrategy is particularly attractive for nonstate crazy units, since it may be the only substrategy with any hope of success.

Straightforward provocations in which the crazy state is a visible provocator is also sometimes a useful substrategy, in that it can provide legitimate occasions for some of the other substrategies and serve as some justification for occupation, destruction, etc. In particular, this may be the case when direct provocation is carefully enacted in coordination with erosion and other substrategies at moments when the target area is highly nervous and may overreact.

Blackmail

Blackmail[4] is a particular substrategy, distinguished by the threat of some horrible consequences if a demand is not complied with. It operates on the element of fear, in addition to benefit-cost considerations. Threats to shoot hostages and to blow up captive airplanes are contemporary illustrations. Blackmail appears to be a very effective substrategy, with particular significance for (a) the more extreme cases of crazy nonstate units who have very limited military external-action capabilities; and (b) martyr crazy states with nuclear instruments. It is technically very easy to hit high-value targets through terrorist tactics requiring little more than chemical explosives and committed persons ready to sacrifice themselves. A particular feature is that through carefully selected action, the blackmailer can achieve impact which is disproportional to his total external-action capabilities.

A main feature of blackmail is the seemingly great disproportion between the punishment promised in case the demands are not complied with and the demand itself, for instance the threat that many hostages will be executed unless some prisoners are released. If both of them are of equal value for the target multiactor, motives to give in to blackmail are strongly reduced—though anxiety and fear may induce submission. Another essential condition is credibility—but this is not very difficult to achieve in respect to infraconventional blackmail devices.

Important is the possibility of indirect blackmail, that is blackmail exercised in respect to a third multiactor to make it press the target multiactor to engage in the activity desired by the crazy state. Especially, international powerful multiactors such as the United States serve as attractive means for the exercise of indirect blackmail. A familiar case is the threat to harm a United States citizen unless the United States convinces some country, which is the real target of the crazy state (or, usually, noncountry group) to do some act, such as release political prisoners and pay ransom.

Blackmail through promise of credible terror directed at high-value objectives is a substrategy hard to counter when subversive and hidden nonstate units are involved, because deterrent, counterterror, and punishment are hard to apply unless the blackmailers are exposed by successful intelligence. The situation is different for a crazy state which tries to blackmail. Here, blackmail may be a catalyst for countercraziness strategies—by making the crazy nature of the involved countries obvious. Short-range successes may be counterproductive by convincing the target multiactor and other international multiactors that the crazy state must be restrained. Therefore, for identified countries (or highly visible noncountry units) to engage in blackmail, they must possess means to reduce vulnerability to countercraziness strategies, such as a continuous blackmail capacity which is not exhausted in a few shots.

An extreme illustration of absolute blackmail which clarifies some aspects of a pure blackmail strategy under hypothetical circumstances is a doomsday machine. A credible doomsday machine possessed by an extreme martyr crazy state (recognized as such and credited with preference to blowing itself up rather than not achieving its goals) is a perfect blackmail situation. To avoid branding this illustration as pure science fiction, let the reader consider a Nazi-like regime where the top elite possess a device which approximates a doomsday machine. It is not necessary for such a doomsday machine to endanger the whole world; destruction of main centers is sufficient. If an additional condition is met, namely, that there is no technical possibility for a first strike to annihilate the doomsday machine before it can be activated, then the only rational response is temporary capitulation. Here, we run into mirror effects: capitulation is the only rational response (under some value assumptions which will be explicated later on). Therefore, doomsday machinelike blackmail may be used by multiactors who, if the chips are down, would not activate the device. Therefore, even if capitulation is the only rational response to some threats, it may be in the interest of the target multiactor not to appear always as rational, so as not to encourage blackmail substrategies based on rational reaction by their targets. The doubts whether the blackmailer will realize a threat that endangers his own existence and whether the target multiactor will give in to a threat even if, in terms of benefit-cost, it is instrumental—rational for him to do so—introduce unavoidable uncertainty into strategic analysis. This uncertainty may, on one hand, restrain uses of extreme strategies, such as blackmail; on the other hand, it increases the probability of mistakes of calculations on mutual expectations with possibly catastrophic results for the involved multiactors and for the international system as a whole.

On a less extreme but still very serious level is blackmail with nuclear instruments. If they are possessed by a martyr crazy state and are protected against a preemptive first strike (e.g., a few nuclear bombs hidden in undefined facilities), the target area may have to capitulate. Because of its effectiveness and the difficulties of useful counterstrategies, blackmail is one of the preferable substrategies for crazy states who have a martyr image and suitable military instruments. This applies in particular to (a) nonstate units on the level of terror instruments; and (b) to crazy states on the level of nuclear blackmail.

Occupation

Occupation is more than a substrategy, constituting sometimes a main goal of crazy (and normal) states. Therefore, occupation should often be regarded as the result of successful utilization of other strategies. But sometimes and in some respects, occupation does constitute a substrategy—when occupation is not a goal, but a means for achievement of other goals.

Occupation can proceed in two extreme forms: (1) in stages, as a form of the erosion substrategy; or (2) suddenly, through entry into the target area. The worthwhileness of presenting a target multiactor and his supporters with a *fait accompli* depends (a) on technical feasibility of sudden occupation; (b) on possible retaliatory action; and (c) possible longer-range boomerang effects, such as causing others to recognize the true nature of the crazy state and encouraging effective countercraziness strategies. When effective countercraziness strategies can be avoided or minimized and when it is technically feasible, sudden occupation is often a preferable substrategy, especially in areas which are regarded as outside the domain of concern of the main international multi-actors—such as Central Africa.

According to circumstances, total occupation of the target country often may be preferable to occupation of limited areas (which would leave a bitter adversary). A main consideration is, whether occupation can be sustained for long and at what cost. In other words, can the occupied area be integrated and absorbed—or at least controlled to prevent guerrilla activities and other forms of resistance from growing?

From the point of view of crazy states with proselytizing goals, occupation is a particularly desirable substrategy because it provides more opportunities for conversation than communication and other instruments activated across the border.

Destruction

Destruction can both be an aid to other substrategies and a main substrategy in its own right. As an auxiliary substrategy, destruction can give credibility to blackmail, can serve as a form of provocation, and can deceive some adversaries on the lines of a main future thrust. As a main substrategy, destruction is aimed at causing damage to the target area and advancing the goals of the crazy state. For instance, widespread destruction of transportation or governmental facilities can be a main substrategy for crazy substate units who want to undermine a regime, create turmoil, and break up an establishment. On the country level, a strong counterforce strike is a form of destruction aimed at destroying the military action capabilities of some other actors. Antipopulation and other antivalue (e.g., against industrial facilities, housing and highly valued national monuments) destruction may try to break a target area's will to fight, though this is often a counterproductive substrategy (as shown by the mass bombings of Germany and Japan during the Second World War). A separate category is genocidelike destruction of large parts of the adversary population or a reduction of the economy of the target area by systematic destruction of production facilities. Here, the rationale is to wipe out an adversary or to reduce him to an impotent international multiactor. At this point, destruction as a substrategy merges with the content of craziness. Genocide of Jews by the Nazis and the aim of some of the Arab countries and noncountry units to destroy Israel are cases where total destruction is a goal (which in turn, requires destruction as a main substrategy).

The capacity of nuclear instruments to destroy target areas in minutes—and in an irreversible fashion—provides novel possibilities for destruction as a substrategy. The irreversible nature of nuclear destruction and its speed make it a preferable substrategy for crazy states which have the instruments available, unless some strong countermeasures seem real to them. In this case, countermeasures must prevent the destruction through making an overwhelming threat of punishment. But this threat will often not be credible. It is one thing for normal international multiactors to warn that use of nuclear instruments will result in radical sanctions involving destruction of the crazy state itself. It is quite another thing when the destruction is *fait accompli* to actually carry out the counterthreat and to destroy the crazy state. We will explore this matter when we discuss preferable countercrazy strategies; but it seems clear that often the threat of counterdestruction is not too credible, and a crazy state could hope to get away with a profession of regret, minor compensations to a few survivors, some formal punishment of a few decision-makers, and similar symbolic actions—while the destroyed adversary will not come to life again. Therefore, unless radical countercraziness strategies are adopted, destruction may emerge as a preferable crazy substrategy.

Timing

Timing is a relevant dimension for all substrategies since the mix in which they are to be combined involves not only combinations of different substrategies at

Table 5-2
Some Preferable Strategies for Possible Crazy States

Preferable Mix of Substrategies

Possible Crazy States	Deception	Infiltration and take-over from within	Conversion	Erosion	Isolation	Alliances	Provocation	Blackmail	Occupation	Destruction	Timing
Crazy propaganda and weak nuclear country	1	0	4	2	2	2	0	1 or 2	0	0	3
Crazy medium nuclear country	2	0	1	2	2	2	1	2 or 3	0	1 or 2	3
Crazy martyr weak nuclear country	2	0	1	2	2	2	2	3	0	3	3
Crazy irrational martyr weak nuclear country	"Preferable strategy" concept does not apply										
Crazy medium infraconventional state	1	4	2	3	1	1	3	3	0	0	3
Crazy martyr Doomsday state	0	0	0	2	1	2	0	4	0	3	1
Crazy irrational martyr Doomsday state	"Preferable strategy" concept does not apply										
Crazy medium conventional country	2	1	1	3	2	2	3	2	4	1	3

Key:
0 not part of preferable mix
1 minor part of preferable mix
2 medium part of preferable mix
3 major part of preferable mix
4 dominant part of preferable mix

any one time, but their ordering in the time dimension. There are some overall features of preferable timing for crazy states which justify treatment as a separate substrategy (through a different one than the others). Thus, a preferable timing substrategy for crazy states is to engage in active operations while the main international multiactors are preoccupied. In particular, periods of intense preoccupation of the supercountries can present unique opportunities for crazy states, though they must consider the possibility that in a major international clash, one or another multiactor may use radical countercraziness strategies which would not be feasible during periods of international tranquility.

Preferable strategies will always consist of some mix of different substrategies, as already pointed out. The mix which is preferable under given circumstances depends on the specific relevant characteristic—which cannot be dealt with meaningfully in generalized and abstract terminology. We have clarified some of the main features of preferable strategies for crazy states in order to understand their nature, their possible behavior, and to design effective countercraziness strategies. But some illustrations of possible preferable strategies which include a mix of the various substrategies may be useful to clarify the nature of crazy states and the complexity of issues which are involved in effective counterstrategies. A few generalized features of preferable strategy mixes for possible crazy states are presented in Table 5-2. This table is insufficient to provide the full flavor of crazy state strategies, because it ignores the dependence of strategies on particular cases, circumstances, counterbehavior by other multiactors, and all the other details of behavior in the real world, and because it is derived in part from the very definitions of the possible crazy states. But it should reveal some features of preferable strategies. It is these preferable strategies and various less extreme manifestations which are the main challenge for countercraziness strategies.

Some Preferable Countercraziness Strategies

From a methodological point of view, the concept of preferable countercraziness strategy is on the same level as the concept of preferable strategy for crazy states, as discussed in Chapter 5.

The characteristics of crazy states are somewhat more defined than the characteristics of the multiactors who engage in countercraziness activities. Therefore, in addition to countercraziness substrategies analogous to the substrategies of craziness discussed in Chapter 5, it is necessary to identify a number of basic countercraziness strategies which substitute for the policy guidelines provided in crazy states by their dimensions of craziness.

Preferable countercraziness strategies apply to all international multiactors who engage in countercraziness behavior. A particular case involves countercraziness strategies adopted by a crazy state against another crazy state with which it is in conflict. Under concrete circumstances, conflict between two crazy states may present some unique features; but for my purposes, countercraziness behavior is examined without distinction whether the multiactors engaged in countercraziness strategies are, themselves, possible crazy states or normal states. A particular mix of basic strategies and substrategies must be designed to fit the particular characteristics of each situation. My analysis is on a general level and is designed to clarify some characteristics of countercraziness strategies without going into details.

The most effective and the most efficient way to handle the possibility of crazy states is (1) to prevent the crazy state from happening; (2) if it happens, to prevent it from getting more crazy; and (3) to prevent it from achieving external-action capabilities. To prevent possible crazy states from being realized constitutes, therefore, the first preferable countercraziness basic strategy.

This basic strategy involves two main substrategies.

*Substrategy 1. Reduce conditions
which encourage crazy states, or which
encourage them to become crazier.*

Insofar as the conditions which increase the probability of realization of crazy states are known, reduction of these conditions presents a preferable countercraziness substrategy. As we saw in Chapter 3, reliable information on the variables increasing the probability of realization of crazy states is not available. Some of the conditions which can be identified and which may encourage realization may be impossible to influence, or they may provide beneficial potential pay-offs which make their prevention impractical. This applies, for instance, to the rapid state of social transformation—which cannot be controlled and which may be regarded to have a potential benefit which justifies the risks of realization of possible crazy states. Nevertheless, even though it is difficult with the present state of knowledge to make this substrategy operative, it deserves emphasis because it provides a guideline for urgently needed research. More important, with respect to particular cases, some of the factors encouraging trends toward crazy states are known; in these cases, reduction is a preferable countercraziness substrategy, unless the costs (in other values) are too high.

An alternative to reducing the factors which may result in the emergence of a crazy state is to engage in active preventive measures, such as control of communication which encourages craziness, restraint of potential crazy leaders, etc. Again, the price in terms of other social values (freedom of communication, etc.) must be carefully compared to the impact of a crazy state.

This substrategy deals not only with the prevention of crazy states, but also with inhibition of their becoming more crazy (see, also, Substrategy 5). Degrees of craziness which should be prevented include movement from (1) unreasonable to counterreasonable goals contents; (2) medium-intensity to high-intensity goal commitment; (3) medium-risk to high-risk propensity; and (4) unaccepted to counteraccepted style. In respect to the means-goals relation dimension, the situation is more complex. Our culture conditions us to assume that an instrumental crazy state is preferable to a counterinstrumental crazy state. But this is not always true—because a counterinstrumental crazy state will be much less effective and efficient in pursuing its goal content and in building up and using its external-action capabilities.

Ways to prevent a crazy state from becoming crazier may involve reduction of the factors resulting in such changes (if known and manipulatable) or haste in applying countercraziness strategies to do away with the basis for becoming more crazy.

*Substrategy 2. Reduce conditions
for development of external-action
capabilities by possible crazy states.*

If Substrategy 1 was hard to make operational, Substrategy 2 is somewhat easier to execute. In principle, it is quite clear what should be done in order to reduce the probability of possible crazy states developing a significant external-action capability. The flow of knowledge and the flow of hardware which are essential to build up external-action capabilities must be restrained, controlled, and monitored. This necessity is readily recognized in respect to nuclear weapons and nuclear technology, even though the way in which it is being handled does not provide much basis for optimism regarding this countercraziness substrategy. In principle, the operational meanings of controlling availability of nuclear, infraconventional, ultraconventional, and conventional weapons; and of the know-how, and the hardware required for their production—are at least concrete. Again, a price is sure to be involved. Thus, for instance, even as commercial reactors using enriched uranium become economically preferable, it may be better to forgo economic advantages in order to restrain their proliferation.

The costs of controlling access to information, and interfering, to some extent, with freedom of flow of scientific knowledge, and freedom to study different subjects in other countries must be recognized. Indeed, the need to control flow of information in order to reduce the probability of possible crazy states building up a significant external-action capability is a good illustration of required changes in basic frames of appreciation[a] if crazy states are to be avoided. I will return to such required changes in basic frames of appreciation later.

The overall basic strategy to prevent conditions which encourage crazy states (and establishment of external-action capabilities) becomes more focused when signs of emergence of a crazy state can be discerned. Basic strategy 2 is directed at the situation when a possible crazy state begins to emerge. In such a case, a preferable basic strategy is to discourage and hinder the beginning crazy state from developing an external-action capability.

This basic strategy has a number of substrategies, which are very important because of the relative ease of handling crazy states in *status nascendi*. It is still easy to deal with them because the crazy states are not yet fully established and have not yet a significant external-action capability (in some cases, at least). Also, it may be more feasible to activate countercraziness strategies for specific states which show indicators of craziness than it is to activate diffuse countercraziness preventive measures without discrimination all over the world. This applies, for instance, to nuclear proliferation, where differentiation between normal states and going-crazy states may be indicated.

Substrategies 3, 4, and 5 belong to the basic strategy to handle crazy states when they begin to emerge.

---

[a]Frames of appreciation include all factors shaping a person's judgment about the world and what to do about it. In addition to tacit theories (discussed in Chapter 1), frames of appreciation include values, concepts, motives, predictions, etc.[1]

Substrategy 3. Early detecting of emerging possible crazy states.

Early detection and identification of emerging crazy states is most important to permit specific countercraziness measures. In order to detect emerging crazy states, two conditions must be met: (1) a perceptive framework to recognize the possibility of crazy states and to draw conclusions from early symptoms must exist; and (2) useable indicators of emerging craziness must be developed.

History provides illustrations of signs of craziness, which, in retrospect, seem obvious to us, but which were ignored (even though the signs were correctly received). This blindness was usually caused by the absence of an interpretative framework which recognized the possibility of craziness and which searched for early indicators of emerging craziness. The development of Nazi Germany into a crazy state and—on a more tactical level—preparations for the attack on Pearl Harbor[2] are good illustrations of situations where indicators were available in public and were, indeed, presented loudly and clearly by Hitler, himself. The majority of international multiactors and their policymakers refused to listen to those signs because of the absence of a frame of appreciation which recognized the possibility of craziness. Therefore, existence of a perceptive framework which recognizes the possibility of craziness and looks for its signs is an essential requisite.

Also needed, on a more technical level, are indicators of emerging craziness which can be identified, both by open and by clandestine intelligence activities. In part, the task of early identification of crazy states is not too difficult because of the inherent characteristics of craziness which make camouflage difficult. In particular, ideologies are hard to camouflage. The problem lies in the opposite direction: of discriminating between ideologies which seem crazy but have no real significance and ideologies and other characteristics which signify a real crazy state.

A conservative posture which prefers to overestimate the probabilities and which is willing to take precautionary measures on the basis of inconclusive symptoms may help solve the identification problem and make the task of early detection easier. To build up a set of indicators of propensity-for-craziness, many variables must be included, e.g., analyses of school books and contents of cultural material, indoctrination literature used in the armed forces, military contingency plans, changes in domestic politics, and so on. Special attention must be given to development of external-action capabilities which go beyond the traditional military-balance contents, including, in particular, image manipulation communication capabilities, nuclear instruments, and infraconventional and ultraconventional instruments. Some of the indicators are susceptible to strict quantitative treatment, others will be more qualitative and impressionistic.

None of the indicators, by itself, is very reliable. But with the help of sets of such indicators, trends towards craziness can be detected and identified early—if an effort is made to develop indicators and if a readiness to accept their conclusions exists.

The next three substrategies depend upon early detection; they are designed to discourage and hinder crazy states in *status nascendi*.

Substrategy 4. Activate particular controls
to hinder emerging crazy states from
developing a significant external-action
capability.

The general recommendation presented in Substrategy 2 to reduce conditions permitting establishment of an external-action capability applies, in particular, to states which show indications of moving in the direction of craziness. Specific action includes embargoes on knowledge and hardware which are significant for building up external-action capability, specially nuclear material, and nuclear information. Also needed are restraints on conventional, infraconventional, and ultraconventional information and hardware. With respect to states which show signs of moving in the direction of craziness, more extreme steps are justified than the diffuse and preventive ones proposed in preferable Substrategy 2. When a state shows movement in the direction of craziness, there is no justification for balancing the economic and political costs of refusing the export of knowledge and materials to it. The necessity to prevent a crazy-going state from building significant external-action capabilities must receive priority. Even if the claim is made that imposing embargoes increases propensity to craziness, the dangers of having a crazy state develop a significant external-action capability may often outweigh the risks. It is particularly important to prevent the crazy state from crossing a number of thresholds which could make it very powerful in terms of external-action capabilities. Of these, the nuclear is the single most important one. To prevent a crazy state from developing any nuclear weapons—is, therefore, a main goal of this substrategy. To prevent a crazy state from building up significant ultraconventional military instruments is another main goal. Most important of all, a crazy state must be prevented from moving in the direction of doomsday machines; and, on a slightly less, but still very, critical level, a crazy state must be prevented from building up advanced nuclear capabilities. (But each situation must be carefully considered to decide whether having second-strike capability reduces the advantage of a first-strike destruction-oriented substrategy for some crazy states.)

Implied in recommended preferable Substrategy 4 are (a) the ability and desire to differentiate between different countries and various noncountry units with respect to restraints on information and hardware; and (b) the ability to impose embargoes which have a strong impact on the state's capacity to get relevant hardware and information. The second condition implies some degree of cooperation between supercountries and other major suppliers.

*Substrategy 5. Reverse trend toward
craziness.*

This, again, is a particular application of Substrategy 1 to states which already show indications of moving toward craziness. When a country begins to show signs of becoming crazy (and the same applies to noncountry units), concrete steps to reverse the trend are indicated, including infiltration and take-over from within, and other forms of interference (such as efforts to influence economic conditions which encourage craziness, efforts to change the elite if it shows tendencies toward craziness, etc.). This involves various degrees of intervention which, in turn, requires abandonment of traditional concepts of sovereignty.

One form of intervention which deserves mention is provision of aid to a normal government endangered by possible take-over by a crazy party, crazy faction, crazy movement or some other internal crazy unit. Preventing take-over by such a crazy unit is a convenient way to reduce the probability of emergence of crazy countries. The difficulty is that every government endangered by an opposition will appeal for help, claiming that the opposition will make the country into a crazy state if permitted to take it over. This may result in a very conservative status-quo power structure similar to the aftermath of the Congress of Vienna. This raises not only hard problems of value preferences, but also the possibility that by helping the repression of innovative forces, one helps them become more radicalized and really crazy, while if they had been permitted to take over the government at less costs, they would have lost their fervor and become normalized. Careful monitoring to limit interventions only to cases where really crazy units may take over a country can provide some help in handling this dilemma. But it is clear that insofar as my main analysis on the dangers of crazy states under conditions of emerging weapons technology is correct, priority should be given in doubtful cases to prevention of crazy states, even if such a policy slows down some needed political transformations in some countries.[3] But much care should be taken to keep such an intervention policy from being misused for other purposes.

*Substrategy 6. Avoid encouraging
craziness by rewarding it.*

The necessity to avoid actions which encourage craziness by rewarding it should be emphasized. It is particularly important to avoid encouraging craziness by giving in to it. Illustrations are provided by some tendencies to give in to aircraft hijacking and kidnapping by noncountry crazy units. (Though lately, there is more readiness to stand up to such blackmail.) In each case, giving in to crazy demands seems, on first look, preferable to innocent persons being killed. But when we take into account the possibility of craziness developing and being imitated because of success, then the individual cases of crazy demands should no longer be considered exclusively in terms of the costs and benefits of that case, alone. The impact (on accelerated movements towards craziness and an increasing number of crazy demands) which results from giving in to single demands must be considered. In general, one should not give in to crazy states, and, in particular, to blackmail strategies. From a long-range point of view, it is often preferable to pay some price now rather than a much larger and even more cruel price later. True, this is a difficult consideration when real persons are involved. But the difficulties of normal states to face up to crazy states (because the normal states deal with crazy behavior in terms of accepted morality) involve too large a cost in possible future human suffering to be morally acceptable. When crazy behavior is confronted, the response must not be decided upon in terms of a short-range benefit-cost analysis in which immediate gains outweigh future considerations. The repression and reversal of craziness to avoid future catastrophes must be the main guideline. The only exceptions are when acceding to demands (1) may defuse the factors resulting in craziness; or (2) when time can be bought to prepare decisive countercraziness measures.

Substrategy 7. Counterbalance emerging crazy states.

Counterbalancing is an important countercrazy substrategy to reduce propensities towards craziness and to limit its impact. It involves building up superior capabilities which will contain the emerging crazy state and, hopefully, reduce its propensity to craziness by showing the futility of its goals—and thus encourage anticraziness factions in the crazy state itself. This substrategy involves encouraging local alliances directed against the emerging crazy state and supplying its potential adversaries with equipment and external-action capabilities to fight the crazy state and to deter it.

Strengthening potential target multiactors is important in order to localize the impact of emerging crazy states and to minimize implications for the international system, including involvement of the supercountries. In more traditional terminology, it is preferable to preserve local stability by making sure that the countercrazy states possess the more powerful external-action capabilities (not to be mixed up with "balance of power," which is too weak to stop crazy states). This substrategy is particularly attractive insofar as it may restrain crazy states from having more than local impact. At the same time, the limits of any local countercraziness strategy should be recognized. Main limits stem (a) from the already-mentioned "illusion of distance"; and (b) from the present structure of the international system, which makes it hard to keep supercountries and major countries out of local conflict. Despite these difficulties, counterbalancing crazy states by strengthening their adversaries is one of the more feasible countercrazy strategies.

We now reach the stages when a possible crazy state is no longer in *status nascendi*, but exists as a fully crazy multiactor. Here, the first need is to actively confront the crazy state and weaken it. The basic strategy of actively confronting and weakening existing crazy states depends, in its operational details (as do the other basic strategies and substrategies) on the concrete circumstances, and, in particular, on the external-action capabilities of the specific crazy state. Especially difficult are cases of noninstrumental crazy states, of martyr crazy states, and of crazy supercountries. Leaving aside problems of adjusting preferable basic strategies and substrategies to concrete circumstances, it is possible to identify the following main preferable substrategies within basic strategy 3.

Substrategy 8. Deter crazy states.

The idea of deterring crazy states is a particularly appealing one, because of the very high effectiveness of deterrence and because of the popularity of deterrence as a preferable strategy (thanks to the deterrence balance between the two supercountries and the widespread adoption of deterrence concepts in strategic studies and practice). Therefore, it is all the more necessary to identify and pinpoint the weaknesses of deterrence as a useful countercraziness strategy, before recommending it as a preferable substrategy under carefully delineated circumstances.

In confronting crazy states, the concept of deterrence must be circumscribed as described in the following paragraphs.

A. Deterrence assumes some instrumental rationality in the defined sense of means-goals relation. If a crazy state is noninstrumental, then deterrence is inapplicable because the promise of sanctions will not influence behavior. This is even more so when we get into cases of counterinstrumental behavior, when the absence of relationships between means and goals makes any threat of punishment irrelevant.

B. Credibility is also a difficult requirement when confronting crazy states. Credibility is a matter of images, and images are shaped by ideology. Therefore, because a crazy state has intensely held ideologies which influence and shape and distort its perceptions, the most determined countercrazy multiactor may not seem credible. Reliance on actions which make deterrence credible in the eyes of normal multiactors cannot be relied upon when crazy states are confronted.

C. Because of the particular goals of crazy states, their utility functions are significantly different from those of normal states[b] (by definition). Therefore, deterrence through threatening punishments directed at values and targets which seem important to the deterring country may be quite irrelevant for the crazy state. Thus, the threat of boycott may be seen as a welcome aid in isolating the country from influence by others and increasing the threat perception in the eyes of the population. Even limited military threats of isolated strikes may help a crazy state mobilize its population by confirming the image of the external world which it wants to sell to its population. Similarly, human life may have quite a different value for a crazy state than for a normal state; therefore, a threat of loss of human life would have much less significance than the deterrers think.

D. One of the basic characteristics of crazy states is a different risk propensity, with tendencies to high-risk policies. Therefore, the assumption that some probability of punishment is sufficient to deter—just does not apply.

It is necessary to redesign deterrence so that it can serve as a substrategy for countercrazy action. Even when redesigned, deterrence is useless *vis-a-vis* counterinstrumental crazy states and *vis-a-vis* extreme cases of martyr crazy states, (not to speak about counterinstrumental martyr crazy states). With the exception of such extreme prototypes which hardly ever exist in reality, deterrence can constitute a useful countercraziness substrategy, if it meets the description described below.

(1) Deterrence must aim at values highly regarded by the crazy state. This will often require a massive deterrence threat aimed at large parts of its population, and, in particular, at the ruling elite. This can be achieved either by threatening a very massive and comprehensive deterrence threat, such as nuclear countercity strike, or by threatening a selective deterrent capability which can hit the main leaders personally.[4] Especially interesting is the second possibility, because of its high effectiveness in deterring some crazy states while causing only low damage to innocent human beings. The difficulty with it is that it requires counterstylistic patterns of conflict by the involved normal multiactor and needs some international support—and these are not requirements easy to meet.

(2) Credibility has to be achieved through obvious actions that cannot be

---

[b]There are great differences between normal states, for example, with respect to the evaluation of human life and tolerance to pressure and losses.

ignored even by highly biased ideologically shaped perceptions of reality. Therefore, declarations and minor symbolic acts cannot relied upon to establish credibility for a massive countercraziness deterrence. Exemplary attacks, demonstration blasts, and similar counterstylistic measures may be required to establish credibility.

(3) It is not enough that deterrence should be perceived as possible or even highly probable. Deterrence has to be assured, especially when the involved crazy state has a high-risk propensity. Visible irreversible commitments to undertake defined actions in clearly identified circumstances are, therefore, required—in line with Thomas Schelling's concept of visible thresholds and automated reactions.[5] Because of the differences in culture between crazy and normal states, no tacit signals can be relied upon. Rather, when we confront crazy states, it is essential to convince them of massive overkill deterrence through irreversible and highly visible measures so that we can stop them without having to realize our threats.

When these three conditions are met, but only when they are met, deterrence may be a preferable countercrazy substrategy. When those conditions are not met, deterrence is a counterproductive strategy—because it may mislead one into believing that deterrence is working and that therefore no further preparations for collision need be made.

Substrategy 9. Actively and intensely
pursue reinforced versions of
Substrategies 4, 5, and 6.

Once a crazy state exists, action to limit its external-action capabilities, action to try to reverse craziness, and action to avoid encouragement for crazy action—are all the more important. Once craziness exists, Substrategies 4, 5, and 6 should be pursued in a more intense form, with complete embargo on military information and hardware, complete avoidance of craziness-encouraging action, and more active and costly efforts to reverse craziness, including intense efforts to infiltrate and take-over from within.

Substrategy 10. Prepare local
multiactors for countercraziness action.

This, too, is a more intense version of an earlier substrategy, namely, Substrategy 7. But once a crazy state exists, counterbalance is insufficient. It is necessary not only to stop development of craziness, but to reverse the nature of the crazy state. Preferably, to avoid international repercussions, this should be achieved through localized activity, involving, first, craziness isolation through counter-craziness alliances; and, later, active penetration of the crazy country and reversal of its nature. Providing the local multiactors with the necessary external-action capability and reinforcing their internal political system so it can withstand and confront craziness are essential. This substrategy is especially significant because it is designed to roll back craziness and to avoid diffusion of it.

Care must be taken not to supply external-action capabilities to multiactors who might join the crazy state later. Therefore, aid in building countercraziness capabilities in local multiactors must be accompanied by careful monitoring to avoid any trends towards craziness. Local control must prevent resources from falling into the hands of the crazy states—either because the latter succeeded in taking over the relevant multiactor, or because the local multiactor was converted by devious means such as theft, bribary, etc.

Substrategy 10 leads us directly into the next basic strategy, which puts forth the proposition that crazy states must be incapacitated. This applies, in particular, to very dangerous crazy states, including martyr crazy countries with any nuclear or ultraconventional external-action capability. Because of the high dangers involved in crazy states which combine high degrees of craziness with powerful external-action capabilities, it is necessary to incapacitate them before they can do irreversible harm. But this master policy must be pursued carefully, because of the possibility that when powerful crazy states are involved, any effort to incapacitate them may result in destruction and other negative effects that are as bad as those that may be caused at the initiative of that crazy state. Therefore, under such circumstances, any real possibility of a given crazy state becoming normal again without causing too much damage may sometimes be preferable to the certainty of losses involved in attempts to incapacitate it. These two sides of the balance must be carefully examined, before incapacitation activities are undertaken. Much depends upon (1) available technology; and (2) how much of an incapacitation effort can be undertaken and yet keep the damage caused by the crazy state before it is incapacitated to bearable limits. Damage caused to innocent human beings in the crazy state, itself, are, also a variable to be taken into account. Another relevant consideration involves the long-range impact on propensity-to-craziness if radical incapacitation steps are or are not undertaken. Subject to these hedgings, which apply, in particular to major countries that become crazy, incapacitation is a basic strategy of utmost importance. It is the basis for Substrategies 11 to 14.

Substrategy 11. Destroy
external-action capability.

This is an essential step once a crazy state has strong martyr tendencies and very aggressive goal contents, coupled with a high (but not extreme) level of external-action capabilities. A decisive counterforce strike is what is recommended by Substrategy 11. The purpose is to reduce the external-action capability of the crazy state to a lower level, both as a countercraziness step, by itself, and as a main step on the way to reversal of the crazy state and its transformation into a normal state. The external-action capabilities required for a successful counterforce strike depend on the capabilities of the crazy state. Counterforce nuclear strike, sabotage, airborne strike, conventional spot bombing—these are only some illustrations of possible counterforce strike forms which are preferable under concrete circumstances. Even if the counterforce strike is not expected to destroy all or most of the external-action capability, such a counterstrike may, nevertheless, constitute a preferable substrategy if the crazy state is expected, in any case, to use its external-action capability. If significant parts of a crazy state's external-action capability are expected to survive a counterforce strike, then suitable action must be taken toward limiting damage from its expected reactions.

Substrategy 12. Stimulate revolt.

Stimulation of revolt, if feasible, may constitute a preferable countercraziness substrategy designed to incapacitate a crazy state. The trouble is that in more advanced states, feasibility of organizing internal revolts is very low. Nevertheless, this possibility must be borne in mind.

Substrategy 13. Occupy crazy state.

Whether in itself, or whether combined with Substrategies 11 and 12, occupation of a crazy state may be unavoidable for real incapacitation of it. Recognizing the necessity to occupy a crazy state in order to reduce its external-action capability and to enforce transformation is essential in order to reduce the cost of such occupation, both for the occupiers and for the innocent population. In particular, initiation of occupation at a time chosen by the countercrazy multiactors and not by the crazy state, is essential for making occupation a low-cost operation. The mix of external-action instruments to be used for most effective occupation depends on the particular circumstances of the case, not permitting any *a priori* valid generalizations. But recognition of the absolute necessity of occupying some of the possible crazy states should result in (a) preparation of suitable countercraziness external-action instruments; (b) development of suitable operation plans; and (c) initiation of occupation in ways that reduce its costs. More important is the political and moral legitimation of the necessity to occupy crazy countries; this belongs to the need for changes in the basic frames of appreciation, to which I will return.

Substrategy 14. Limit damage that
can be caused by crazy state.

An integral part of the basic strategy of incapacitating a crazy state is to reduce the damage which it can cause. Preferable damage limitations should be used in combination with counterforce strike, revolt organization, and occupation—the intention being to reduce the damage which will be caused during the armed clash. But the main substrategies of counterforce strike and occupation may be unfeasible due to internal political reasons in the multiactors and because of the international situation. Therefore, damage limitation with respect to possible crazy states emerges sometimes as the only feasible substrategy available to various multiactors. The advantage of this substrategy is that it can be developed in the absence of a visible threat. (This substrategy is also convenient because some steps useful to limit possible damages from crazy states are also useful for limiting damage from conflict with normal multiactors.) Indeed, the very recognition of the possibility of crazy states and, even more so, of early signs of some development in the direction of emergence of craziness—should serve to encourage intensive damage limitation activities. These, in the longer run, will reduce the threat of crazy states by minimizing the damage they can cause. These will also serve to meet an essential prerequisite for more active counterstrategies.

The details of damage limitation *vis-a-vis* possible crazy states depend on circumstances and are, in fact, not too dissimilar from the problems of defense and damage limitation in conflict between normal states. But a unique characteristic is the nonstylized and counterstylized dimensions of crazy state behavior. When facing crazy states, counterstylistic action must be expected, ranging from clandestine nuclear attack to taking hostages. Here, we meet one of the limits on damage limitation as a countercraziness strategy: because of the nonstylized nature of the behavior of many crazy states, their modes of causing damage are too diversified and too innovative to permit damage limitation without intolerable interference with regular life in their potential target multiactors. It is one thing to build up an ABM system. It is a completely different thing to install close control on all public places to detect possible attempts to plant bombs. Therefore, in many respects, maximum feasible defense and damage limitation is limited, and active steps to incapacitate crazy states are often the only effective way to limit damage caused by them. Nevertheless, damage limitation is, in part, feasible and can be very useful in benefit-cost terms. The possibilities of installing antihijacking devices and antihijacking routines in aircraft illustrate such a case where active countercraziness substrategies seem difficult and damage limitation is relatively easier. Even in respect to a limited nuclear attack, damage can be reduced through suitable preparations. Therefore, whether by itself or as a component of a package of countercraziness strategies, countercraziness damage limitation is one of the more important substrategies available.

When very crazy states with highly developed external-action capabilities appear, another basic strategy may be called for, namely, accommodation. When confrontation of a crazy state is clearly suicidal, then accommodation leading up to capitulation may constitute a rationally preferable basic strategy. This basic strategy ignores a critical moral issue, namely, When is it better to be dead than to be alive? If we prefer living even enslaved (hopefully, temporarily) to being dead, then accommodation may be least catastrophic (and, therefore, preferable) under some circumstances, such as the hypothetical case of a martyr crazy state with doomsday capabilities. When death is preferred, then, of course, this basic strategy has little appeal. Assuming that basic values prefer life to death, even when life is miserable, then there are two preferable substrategies within this basic strategy.

Substrategy 15. Bargain to win time.

Insofar as it is possible to delay catastrophe, through bargaining and limited giving in, these alternatives represent the worst at its best. Stalling, partial giving in, symbolic capitulation unaccompanied by real consequences, verbal gratification of the requirements of the crazy state—these are some of the devices which may be useful for bargaining with a crazy state. For facing the more extreme crazy states, such bargaining may be of little avail—though, because some of the goal contents of craziness are symbolic, much can be achieved under some circumstances by symbolic capitulation, such as nominal adjustment of institutions and values to the demands, and careful deception. Because the worst is expected, the possible negative consequences of being caught in deception are tolerable for society, though individuals must be ready to sacrifice themselves.

Substrategy 16. Capitulate.

Capitulation presents the ultimate giving-in to craziness. It is only to be considered after all other substrategies fail and if it does not involve giving up values which one holds more dearly than survival, itself. Indeed, the readiness to sacrifice oneself in order to resist crazy states is a main asset necessary in order to stop them. Therefore, the very consideration of capitulation is disfunctional, unless a really extreme case of crazy state with very strong external-action capability, is ready to put the target multiactor to the final test—survival with capitulation, or total destruction. Even under those circumstances, capitulation should only be regarded as an intermediate phase to be accompanied by efforts to destroy the crazy state later on, from within. Therefore, such a capitulation substrategy should be accompanied with various activities to build up an underground working against the crazy state and directed towards its ultimate defeat, reversal, and—if nothing else works—destruction. All these hedgings may sweeten the capitulation substrategy somewhat; nevertheless, its defeatist content must be recognized. But logical completeness requires that it be mentioned as the last resort in some hypothetical situations. It is the purpose of all other substrategies to avoid reaching a situation where capitulation is the only remaining alternative to complete self-destruction.

As with respect to the preferable strategies for crazy states, so the preferable countercrazy strategies have to be used in different mixes depending on concrete circumstances. But the principle issues have, I think, been clarified.

Realization of the various preferable countercraziness basic strategies and substrategies depends on two different sets of conditions: (1) conditions dealing with the basic frames of appreciation of the relevant countercraziness multi-actors; and (2) conditions with respect to their external-action capabilities.

Especially important and hard to meet are the requirements with respect to frames of appreciation, including, in particular, the following items (some of which have already been mentioned).

(1) Readiness to recognize the possibility of crazy states and to take action which is directed against them, even before they become a visible threat.

(2) Readiness to pay a short-range price in order to avoid the longer-range threat of possible crazy states.

(3) Overcoming of traditional concepts of international relations, including, in particular, the concepts of (a) sovereignty; and (b) equality of countries.[6] Most countercraziness preferable strategies involve intervention in the so-called domestic affairs of other countries. Furthermore, many of the

Table 6-1
Mutual Images of Pax Americana-Sovietica.

Image from point of view of United States - Soviet Union	Image from point of view of a major developed country	Image from point of view of a minor developed country	Image from point of view of an underdeveloped country
Only we can assure world peace.	We are also a major country, entitled to participate in global government.	We are a small country, but more mature than the super countries — look how they mess things up.	This is all 'a conspiracy of the "haves" to continue to control the world and prolong our misery.
Because of the potential of nuclear and ultra-conventional weapons, small conflicts can damage us and even cause irreversible global damage.	What they really want is to keep us down and avoid any competition to their hegemony.	Soon technology will make us all equal in military strength. They want to preserve inequality — and hide their ambitions behind the mask of global benevolence.	The White Race enters now a new stage of global imperialism marked by obvious collusion between the white super countries — who want to perpetuate their racial oppression.
The United Nations is dominated by a mass (and mess) of countries without responsibility or power.	What ruins the United Nations is the Veto power of the big countries — and now they want to blame us.	There is a global forum available — the United Nations. Only big power intrigues hinder its work. Let us make the United Nations work better — on a basis of real equality between all member states and mutual good will.	The one attempt to achieve international democracy is the United Nations. This is why they want to bury it.
Problems such as pollution and overpopulation endanger us and the world. Their handling requires world leadership, which only we can supply.	They became corrupt and decadent and want all others to become the same.	We are entitled to control our own destiny.	"Pollution," "overpopulation" — these are all nonsense invented to keep us down. Soon they will restrict the energy we may use!
"Sovereignty" is an outdated concept, which does not fit a world of close mutual dependencies.	Sovereignty is to nations what liberty is to individuals. They want to enslave us.	For them we are just pawns to be moved as they wish.	Imperialism is not dead, it only changes its forms. Now they want to hide their aggression behind a facade of words on "mutual dependencies". But we know the truth.
"Equality of states" is obviously a myth, and a dangerous one, at that.	Modern weapons serve as "equalizers." Therefore, they want to prevent us from getting and developing nuclear (and ultraconventional) weapons.	States are equal, just as individuals are. The fact that they have more bombs does not make them any better.	This is a new fascist racism. They regard coloured nations as inferior to whites. But we will show them who is better.
Other countries do not have the necessary perspective to handle global issues. Only we can do so.	We are more objective than the two super countries and we are better equipped to handle problems than those "big brutes."	It is the struggle between big nations which ruins the world. The more power small nations get, the better for the world. If the big countries would break up into smaller ones, this would be all for the better.	Western culture is bankrupt. Artificial efforts to sustain its hegemony are doomed.
Other countries must be restrained from causing the world, their region and themselves damage.	We have heard this before, from all rulers who wanted to conquer the world.	It is true that some countries need restraint — namely the super-powers. It is really true — power corrupts, and super-power corrupts superbly.	They see the writing on the wall, but it will not help them.

A "crazy state" can cause catastrophe. The only way to prevent it is close control of the world.	All this talk about "crazy states" is just a smoke screen. They are "crazy" and want to control the world forever.	History repeats itself, and it is always the small and innocent countries which pay the price for the craziness of the big powers.	Who but a crazy nation can regard the awakening of a new world as crazy?
Others do not need large armies and should not be permitted to have nuclear weapons. We will assure to them justice.	Throughout history, power has changed. It is our turn to become a super country – but they want to stop history and perpetuate their own status.	We are able to protect ourselves; protection by them is worse than none at all.	It is now our turn. They will not stop it.
Therefore, we must establish a just and strong *Pax Americana Sovietica.*	Therefore, we must resist oppression of the world by the two super countries. Let us show we are also strong; let us develop our military might to defend our sovereignty and liberty.	Therefore, let us resist their domination as best we can.	Therefore, let us resist this new oppression. Let us gather strength for the day of reckoning.

Note: These images are presented as probable reactions by opinion leaders and policymakers. Many other reactions are also possible and probable; the images in reality will be very heterogenous.

countercraziness strategies involve discrimination between different countries, according to their propensity to craziness. Readiness to interfere in the domestic affairs of other countries, to force on them some activities and controls destined to prevent craziness, and to discriminate in many matters against countries with a higher propensity for craziness—these are among the required characteristics of a frame of appreciation able to confront crazy states.

(4) General readiness for stylistic innovations, permitting adoption of substrategies which involve novel devices and novel types of actions.

Also required are innovations in external-action capabilities, designed to meet the needs of the various proposed preferable substrategies. But these are of a more technical nature, and, therefore, outside the scope of this book. Let me just emphasize the importance of suitable innovations in command, control, and decision capabilities, in vulnerability reduction, in organization of countercraziness forces and in military doctrines.

More important than the need for novel external-action capabilities and more important than the various required changes in frames of appreciation of individual international multiactors is the reconstruction of the whole international system to enable it to face the possibility of crazy states. If crazy states with significant external-action capability are, indeed, a significant danger, then close cooperation between the two supercountries to prevent them and to handle them if they do emerge is essential.[c] If some major countries are among the candidates for a possible crazy state—as may become the case—then, indeed, cooperation between the two supercountries is absolutely essential. And, not incidentally, cooperation between the two supercountries may perhaps reduce the dangers of either one of them going crazy.

What, in a sense, is involved here are the rudiments of a *Pax Americana-Sovietica*. A good case can be made for the claim that only intense cooperation between the two supercountries can provide real safeguards against the emergence of possible crazy states. But the idea of a *Pax Americana-Sovietica* as a main condition for preferable countercraziness strategies brings up an underlying feature of many of the countercraziness strategies: what appears to one actor as a countercraziness strategy will clearly appear to other actors as a symptom of craziness. To illustrate this point, let me contrast the image of a rudimentary *Pax Americana-Sovietica* as seen by the United States and the Soviet Union, and as seen from the perspectives of some other international multiactors—all of them normal (see Table 6-1).

---

[c] If and when some other countries—such as China—approach supercountry capacities, their cooperation in international countercraziness arrangements becomes essential. In every case, cooperation with the major countries is desirable in order to reduce the possibility of one of them being driven toward a condition of craziness and in order to increase the effectiveness of countercraziness measures.

To conclude our consideration of preferable countercraziness strategies, let me mention again that the interaction between preferable crazy strategies and preferable countercraziness strategies must be borne in mind. As already pointed out in Chapter 5, the question is not only one of consecutive interaction between preferable crazy strategies and preferable countercraziness strategies, but one of interaction between mutual images and mutual expectations. The possibilities for such interaction are infinite, resulting in a rich variety of mixes of preferable basic substrategies and strategies. But the various identified substrategies will constitute the main components of these interaction processes.[d]

Because of the hard conditions required for adoption of preferable countercraziness strategies, the probability that, in reality, preferable counter-craziness strategies will be realized is very low. To be able to make some realistic predictions concerning future situations with possible crazy states, it is necessary to consider some of the variables hindering adoption of preferable counter-craziness strategies.

---

[d]The interested reader can exercise his skill and imagination by constructing various interaction scenarios, or even by simulating the confrontation between crazy and normal states. To avoid the fallacy of misleading concreteness, I have decided against illustration of possible interaction processes with hypothetical scenarios.

7 Expected Countercraziness Behavior

In reality, there is very little chance that the preferable countercraziness strategies presented in Chapter 6 will be realized, or even approximated. The characteristics of policy-making in nearly all contemporary societies include so many barriers that the probability that preferable countercraziness strategies will be adopted is nearly zero. Examination of these barriers is essential to permit some predictions on actual countercraziness behavior. These barriers are, in fact, closely related to the fallacies discussed in Chapter 1, but they are broader and more fundamental.

The main barriers to preferable—and even good—strategic policy-making and their implications for countercraziness strategies are discussed below.

1. Immediate problems drive hypothetical issues out of consideration. Scarcity of resources, (in particular, attention and highly qualified persons) combine with the pressure of current crises to prevent treatment of hypothetical issues. In most organizations, special units set up to consider future contingencies and to engage in look-out functions are, in reality, mobilized to deal with current affairs, as soon as any crisis is perceived. Even if a few isolated units in government or outside government do consider hypothetical issues, they are sure to have no impact on actual policies unless some dramatic events demonstrate that what was considered as hypothetical is, in fact, very real.

   At present, and in the foreseeable future, organizations dealing with strategic issues are overburdened with very pressing immediate issues. Therefore, there is little chance that the hypothetical issues of crazy states can receive any serious consideration, and there is even less chance that significant resources will be allocated for preparing necessary action capabilities for countercraziness strategies. Even single instances of craziness, such as aircraft hijacking and kidnapping, will probably receive a minimal interpretation—being regarded as single exceptional occurrences rather than precursors of a possible widespread trend. Only after a number of shocks caused by craziness occur, will crazy states be recognized as a real problem rather than as a hypothetical one.

2. Preference for low risk. In the United States, it any case, preference for low risk is a dominant characteristic of most policy-making, including strategic

policy-making. It is a result of features of organizational decision-making (such as satisfying, incrementalism, organizational routine and dissonance reduction) and contemporary United States political culture. This feature inhibits adoption of many of the preferable countercraziness strategies, which involve significant risks. Those risks are often lower than the risks of not adopting the proposed strategies; but, nevertheless, they appear as quite risky, and are, therefore, barred by the organizational and political tendencies to follow policies which seem to have initially low risks.

3. Policy conservatism. In general, policies tend to follow the past, with incremental change, at most. After significant shock effects, as have occurred in the United States in respect to some domestic issues, policies become more innovative. But in the international scenery as yet, no shocks strong enough to permit the innovations involved in adopting preferable countercraziness strategies have been perceived.

In respect to countercraziness strategies, the tendency to follow policies of the past with incremental change implies that the more a proposed countercraziness strategy is innovative, the less a chance it has of being adopted. Many of the preferable countercraziness strategies require significant changes in frames of appreciation, concepts, styles of conflict, and even in accepted morality in normal countries. Therefore, this barrier is an especially insidious one which is sure to prevent approximation of the preferable countercraziness strategies (at least until significant shocks occur and result in a radical increase in policy innovation).

4. Domestic political constraints. Another very important barrier to preferable countercraziness strategies is domestic political constraints, which put many of the recommended preferable strategies beyond the domain of domestic political feasibility. This is, at present, clearly the case in the United States. But similar variables operate in other countries in different ways, but not necessarily with less impact.

Particularly relevant are domestic political constraints on investments in countercraziness external-action capabilities, on innovations involved in preferable countercraziness strategies and, in general, on true perception of the real nature of crazy states. Internal political constraints can also be viewed as one of the underlying reasons for most of the other barriers.

5. Contemporary characteristics of the international system. The conflict-oriented multivector structure of the contemporary international system all but forecloses possibilities for realization of the more important countercraziness strategies. In particular, the bipolar structure—and, even more so, the movement toward a multipolar structure—of the international power map increases the possibilities for crazy states to gain support from one or another major multiactor. At the very least, countercrazy strategies are inhibited by

the implications of such strategies: preferable countercraziness strategies may interfere with other needs and goals of the multiactors. Multiactors may therefore prefer to take the risks of a crazy state emerging rather than give up what they regard as their overall interests. The widespread subscription to the idea of national sovereignty and of formal equality between all states is an additional impediment to many of the countercraziness strategies. The *modus operandi* of the United Nations illustrates this barrier in operation, precluding effective action against most crazy states. The fears of small and medium countries, and especially third-world countries, that slogans of countercraziness action may be justification for world domination by one or the other supercountry (or possibly, by both of them together) illustrate the unsuitability of the present international system for realization of countercraziness strategies.

To generalize somewhat more, the characteristics of contemporary strategic policy-making are a barrier to preferable countercraziness strategies. Usually, strategic policies are arrived at through a process of zero policy-making, (that is, policy formation through a set of minor and ad hoc decisions which add up to a policy, which was never considered as a whole)[1] and intense conflict between different organizations within a high-pressure environment. Trends of bureaucratic behavior toward satisfying, incremental change, ritualistic fixation, preoccupation with fire extinguishing, innovation repression, etc. inhibit preferable strategies.[a]

The various fallacies of strategic studies in the United States (and in most other countries) must be added to these barriers. In particular, the convex mirror effect masks the crazy state problem.

Taken together, all these factors make it a certainty that none of the preferable countercraziness strategies will be approximated in reality unless some significant changes in strategic policy-making occur. Such changes may, in part, occur thanks to improvement of the policy-making system and/or learning following initial contacts with crazy states. But probably the various barriers will inhibit any real approximation of preferable countercraziness strategies for a long period.

The implications are clear: usually crazy states will be confronted with a

---

[a]It is important to note that the various findings on the weaknesses of organizational decision-making are based on the study of average organizations, especially those in the United States. These findings do not necessarily apply to crusading organizations which are staffed by people motivated by very strong commitments to values. Therefore, the possibility exists that under some circumstances, crazy states may have a somewhat higher propensity to approximate their preferable strategies than their normal adversaries might have. This may be a transitory phenomenon limited to some areas of decision-making—but this possibility is sufficient to aggravate the problems posed by possible crazy states.[2]

mixture of contemporary policies, appeals to abandon craziness, and, occasionally, brilliant but sporadic improvisations. After experience with real cases of crazy states, there may occur a rapid learning period (depending on the intensity of the experience and on the learning capacities of the policy-making systems). Hopefully, dangerless shocks by minor crazy states will result in sufficient learning to permit suitable strategies to be adopted in time. But this is an optimistic view.

Unless significant changes in strategic policy-making occur, expected counter-craziness strategies must, therefore, be expected to be quite ineffective.

8 Significance of the Crazy States Issue

Upon the basis of our examination, we are now equipped for a reevaluation of the significance of crazy states for the international system and its different multiactors.

The central concept for evaluating the significance of possible crazy states for the international system and its multiactors is the concept of "Expected Impact Significance" (EIS). Expected impact significance equals probability of occurrence multiplied by impact if it occurs. Or

$$EIS = p \cdot i.$$

At least aphoristically, this concept should emphasize the necessity to consider and prepare oneself for events which, while of very low probability, may be significant, if they should occur. This concept also explains why limiting attention to high-probability events only is dangerous, because of its neglect of very significant (even if very low probability) events.

The probability of occurrence of possible crazy states was explored in Chapter 3, with the conclusion that crazy states cannot be excluded from what may happen, and that by all available indicators (which admittedly, are inadequate), there exists a probability of more than zero that some possible crazy states will occur in reality. The question of what constitutes the probability threshold beyond which we should regard crazy states as a significant issue—depends on the impact of possible crazy states if and when they should occur. If the impact of a possible crazy state is to destroy humanity, then even a very, very low probability of, let me say, less than one in a thousand, results in a very high expected-impact significance. Less extreme cases of possible crazy states have a lower impact and therefore require a higher probability in order to institute significant problems—but less extreme cases have a higher probability of occurring.

When speaking on the impact of crazy states if they occur, it is necessary to distinguish between impact on different multiactors. The same crazy state may have quite different impacts on some of its direct neighbors, on the region within which it is located, on particular main international multiactors such as the United States, and on the international system as a whole.

To illustrate, let me consider a few main impacts of crazy states on the

97

United States. (A parallel analysis with somewhat different conclusions can be made from the point of view of other multiactors.)

1. Since it is one of the supercountries, United States citizens, assets, and diplomatic representatives are present in all countries and all main regions. Therefore, even highly localized crazy states will indirectly hit and endanger United States property and United States personnel. Furthermore, even assuming no direct concern of the crazy states with the United States, the very presence of United States personnel and property and the very power enjoyed by the United States makes those persons and property convenient leverage points to be used by the crazy states for its purposes, for instance, blackmail. Using United States citizens as hostages by noncountry crazy units is a prime example of this possibility.

2. Beyond the use of locally situated United States personnel and property as a leverage point in the struggle between the crazy states, its target multiactor and other local multiactors, to influence United States involvement in local activities is a main substrategy of the crazy states and the other involved multiactors. As indicated in Chapter 5, isolation of the target area from the support of other international multiactors and enlistment of help are among the preferable substrategies of crazy states. As we have seen in Chapter 5, involvement of the United States (and other supercountries and major countries) is also an essential countercraziness strategy. Therefore, even localized appearances of crazy states will increase the direct pressures upon the United States to get involved in one way or another. Taking into account the widespread alliance system of the United States, in many cases even localized crazy states will unavoidably get the United States involved—especially if both the crazy state and its adversaries pay much attention to the substrategy of getting the United States involved on their side.

3. In most cases, the activities of crazy states will involve significant suffering on the local level. Such suffering may create conditions for United States involvement on behalf of humanitarian interests.

The first three points discussed are of relatively low-compelling force. They provide strong opportunities and pressures for the United States to become involved in localized appearances of crazy states, but involvement may be resisted. Readiness to tolerate some losses in persons and property, to ignore local pressures for help and counterhelp, and local sufferings permit the United States to disregard local phenomena of crazy states. But additional impacts may appear which may be harder to ignore. Such possibilities are discussed below in order of increasing seriousness.

4. In the present international system, many localized occurrences have significance for the global interactions between the two supercountries. In other words, even physically localized phenomena may appear to influence the global balance of powers, at least through influencing the image of the United States, which in turn may influence other features of the United States global posture (such as allies, bases, credibility, voting behavior in the United Nations, etc.). Therefore, localized phenomena may become a challenge to the global posture of the United States.

5. It is possible to imagine changes in the international system which reduce the impact of local and even regional crazy behavior on the United States (and U.S.S.R.) global posture—and indeed such changes may be part of preferable countercrazy strategies. But modern transportation and communication reduce the function of distance as a protection against involvement. Getting the United States involved constitutes both a preferable crazy substrategy and a preferable countercraziness strategy. Therefore, attempts may be made by the crazy state or its adversaries to get the United States involved through direct action *vis-a-vis* the United States, including its mainland. Especially martyr-type crazy states may try to get the United States involved, for instance by camouflaged provocation and terror attacks.

6. Especially serious for the United States, is, of course, a situation in which the United States itself constitutes a target multiactor for possible crazy states. Under historic conditions, this was a nearly impossible contingency: distance and limitations of external-action capabilities combined to inhibit crazy action directly aimed at the United States. But these historic protections do not operate any more. It is not impossible for a crazy state to engage in direct activities *vis-a-vis* the United States (such as through internal terror, clandestine delivery of nuclear weapons and its utilization for terror, provocation, and blackmail). Such increased opportunities for direct crazy action may be accompanied by relevant motivations. One type of motive, namely, to get the United States involved as an instrument for local purposes, has already been discussed.

Now, we are concerned with the much more serious case where the United States itself is a target. To realize the probabilities for such a case, the possibility of hostility against the United States must be considered; for instance, possible third-world hostility against the United States as a symbol of affluence and saturation. If we accept (1) that frustration in the underdeveloped countries is going to increase; (2) the possibilities that widespread frustrations and hostilities against modern countries will combine with racial hostilities; and (3) that new technologies may provide easy access to devastating weapons, then the possibility of the United States emerging as a main target must receive serious consideration.

For instance, some medium crazy country in an underdeveloped area which is desperate at its inability to meet its minimum aspirations, may try to adopt a short cut and blackmail the United States to pay penalties for its affluence (obviously achieved through exploitation of the underdeveloped countries, so their ideology will say). If the crazy states are more than minor countries, the possibility of even a nuclear first strike to rid the world of its white, capitalistic exploiter must not be completely ignored. Possible internal developments in the United States increase the risk of blackmail because of the image that the United States may be getting soft, prone to give in to direct pressures, and even susceptible to a devastating first hit. In considering this possibility, one must bear in mind that images and not objective reality may determine the moves of crazy (and normal) states. Such images may be influenced, as already mentioned, by distortions caused by deep commitment to ideologies, which may result in exaggerated interpretations of domestic United States phenomena—which are often overplayed in the media of mass communication.

7. The success of one or two crazy states in achieving even localized goals may have a contagious effect and result in a more widespread appearance of crazy states. In particular, the possibilities of widespread diffusion of new crazy ideologies cannot be ignored. Thus, unless checked, localized crazy phenomena can become widespread and cover sufficient countries to build up a major external-action capability which can directly endanger the United States.

8. The possibility already mentioned in Chapter 3 of a major country and even of the Soviet Union becoming crazy cannot be ignored. (From the point of view of the Soviet Union, the possibility of the United States getting crazy under some conditions cannot be ignored either.) Even minimum probability of the Soviet Union getting crazy constitutes a devastating catastrophy for the United States (and the world as a whole) and thus it deserves the closest attention and constitutes a case of very high expected impact significance (despite its low probability).

The conclusion seems justified that possible crazy states have a very high impact if they occur, not only on their neighbors and region, but on the global system on the whole, and on the United States in particular. Therefore, even if the probability of occurrence is low, the expected impact significance is high. This conclusion applies to the extreme prototypes and to less extreme forms of crazy states.

In the abstract, it is impossible to grade possible crazy states according to their impact if they should happen to occur, because of the multiplicity of conditions, contexts, and other variables which determine the specific impact. But, I think, the conclusion that crazy states may have a sufficiently high impact to make them a significant strategic issue is justified; certainly, they constitute a major and often critical problem for their target multiactors.

The expectation that actual countercraziness strategies will be far off preferability—because of the reasons presented in Chapter 7—may often encourage and aid rather than retard and reverse crazy states. This factor only adds to the significance of the problem. Surely, crazy states will not behave preferably either. But the danger that crazy states may for some time approximate preferable strategies more so than their adversaries and other international multiactors will approximate preferable counterstrategies—is, I think, a real one. This possibility aggravates the crazy state problem by increasing the probability that crazy states may be permitted to develop and even be aided in building up their external-action capabilities.

My overall conclusion is that crazy states constitute a subject deserving close attention. They should be recognized as a potential main danger to humanity and to each and every international multiactor. Certainly, the possibility of crazy states should become a main subject for attention and analysis in strategic studies. Furthermore, and this is the most important implication of this book, the significance of the crazy state issue should be recognized in strategic policy-making, so that some preparations can be made to face that danger. The earlier the possibilities and dangers of crazy states are recognized—the higher the probability of their prevention and containment and the higher the hope that crazy states will not become a main scourge to mankind.

Selected Readings

There are very few books or articles which deal with the crazy state issue. This list of selected readings includes some of the more relevant ones in order to help the interested reader pursue the subject on his own. This list is not a complete bibliography on the subject nor does it include all the works mentioned as references in this book.

The possibility of crazy states (without using this term) is explicitly mentioned and somewhat discussed in Herman Kahn, et al., *War Termination Issues and Concepts* (N.Y.: Hudson Institute, AD 683775, June 1968), reprinted in part in Herman Kahn, "Issues of Thermonuclear War Termination," *Annals of the American Academy of Political and Social Science*, Vol. 392 (November 1970), pp. 133-172; in Herman Kahn and Anthony J. Wiener, *The Year 2000: A Framework for Speculation on the Next Thirty-Three Years* (N.Y.: Macmillan Co., 1967); and in Raymond Aron, *Peace and War: A Theory of International Relations* (London: Weidenfeld and Nicolson, 1966).

Possible underlying factors which may result in crazy states are discussed in a wide range of literature. Directly relevant are, for instance, Konrad Lorenz, *On Aggression* (N.Y.: Bantam, 1967); Samuel Z. Klausner, *Why Man Takes Chances: Studies in Stress-Seeking* (Garden City, N.Y.: Doubleday, 1968); Eric Hoffer, *The True Believer: Thoughts on the Nature of Mass Movements* (N.Y.: Harper & Row, 1951); Hans Toch, *Violent Men: An Inquiry into the Psychology of Violence* (Chicago: Aldine, 1969), and David J. Finlay, Ole R. Holsti and Richard R. Fagen, *Enemies in Politics* (Chicago: Rand McNally, 1967). More diffuse contributions to the subject are represented, for instance, in Leon Bramson and George W. Goethals, ed., *War: Studies from Psychology, Sociology, Anthropology* (N.Y.: Basic Books, 1964) and David J. Singer, *International Politics: Contributions from the Sociological-Psychological Sciences* (Chicago: Rand McNally, 1965).

History is full of cases of crazy states—the Crusades, the Moslem Holy Wars, the Mahadi revolt in the Sudan, the Assassins, some periods after the French Revolution, various multiactors in the Balkans—these are only a few of the relevant instances. But the job of analyzing these phenomena in modern strategic terms has not yet been undertaken and most readers will not wish to study the specialized literature dealing with these cases in historic terms.

Nearer to us are the cases of Nazi Germany and Japan before the Second World War. The best comprehensive book on Nazi Germany in English is still William L. Shirer, *The Rise and Fall of the Third Reich: A History of Nazi Germany*. (N.Y.: Simon and Schuster, 1960). To get a better sense of the scope of Nazi craziness, one should read Ihor Kamenetsky, *Secret Nazi Plans for*

Eastern Europe: A Study of Lebensraum Policies (N.Y.: Bookman Associates, 1961). Much more revealing are the writings of the Nazi ideologists, but most of those have not been translated into English. On Japan, the single most revealing book is, in my opinion, Nobutaka Ike, *Japan's Decision for War: Records of the 1941 Policy Conferences* (Stanford: Stanford University Press, 1967).

Most readers will be interested in more recent happenings which approximate craziness. A good introduction is provided in the collection of essays on "Collective Violence," *The Annals of the American Academy of Political and Social Science*, Vol. 391, pp. 1-176. Student politics and activism is relevant and receives a lot of attention; a good case study is A. Belden Fields, *Student Politics in France: A Study of the Union Nationale des Etudiants de France* (N.Y.: Basic Books, 1970). Another case is discussed in S.M. Lipset and S. Wolin, ed., *The Berkeley Revolt* (Garden City: Anchor Books, 1969). More important for understanding possible crazy trends is anarchism, which is well discussed in George Woodcock, *Anarchism* (Middlesex, England: Penguin Books, 1962). An important French book which has no parallel in English is Roland Gaucher, *Les Terroristes* (Paris: Albin Michel, 1965).

Modern guerrilla movements present another trend which illustrates some facets of craziness. Good introductions are Shalom Endleman, ed., *Violence in the Street* (London: Gerald Duckworth, 1968); Martin Oppenheimer, *Urban Guerrilla* (Middlesex, England: Penguin Books, 1969); and Luis Mercier Vega, *Guerrillas in Latin America: The Technique of the Counter-State* (London: Pall Mall Press, 1969). The inadequacy of stylized response to such phenomena in the United States context is clearly demonstrated in Robin Higham, ed., *Bayonets in the Streets: The Use of Troops in Civil Disturbances* (Lawrence: University Press of Kansas, 1969).

There exists a very extensive literature on internal war, subversion, etc. The interested reader is recommended to start with Nathan Leiter and Charles Wolf, Jr., *Rebellion and Authority: An Analytic Essay on Insurgent Conflicts* (Chicago: Markham Publishing Co., 1970), and to rely on the references in that book as a guide to detailed country studies. To gain a somewhat broader perspective, the reader should study the internal uses of terror in primitive African communities, in Eugene Victor Walter, *Terror and Resistance: A Study of Political Violence* (N.Y.: Oxford University Press, 1969).

Weapon systems and strategies, in addition to terror, for possibly crazy states are discussed in: Nigel Calder, ed., *Unless Peace Comes* (N.Y.: Viking Press, 1968); J.A.C. Brown, *Techniques of Persuasion: From Propaganda to Brainwashing* (Middlesex, England: Penguin Books, 1963); Andrew M. Scott, *The Revolution in Statecraft: Informal Penetration* (N.Y.: Random House, 1968); Feliks Gross, *The Seizure of Political Power in a Century of Revolutions* (N.Y.: Philosophical Library, 1958); Edward Hyams, *Killing No Murder: A Study of*

Assassination as a Political Means (Bristol: Nelson, 1969); and Daniel Ellsberg, *The Theory and Practice of Blackmail* (Santa Monica, California: The Rand Corporation, P-3883, July 1968). Also relevant, though dealing mainly with the United States, is James L. Payne, *The American Threat: The Fear of War as An Instrument of Foreign Policy* (Chicago: Markhan Publishing Co., 1970).

Especially important are the possibilities of nuclear proliferation in crazy states. Good introductions to the subject are: Alastair Buchan, ed., *A World of Nuclear Powers?* (Englewood Cliffs: Prentice-Hall, 1966); William B. Bader, *The United States and the Spread of Nuclear Weapons* (N.Y.: Pegasus, 1968); and R.N. Rosecrance, ed., *The Dispersion of Nuclear Weapons* (N.Y.: Columbia University Press, 1964). Also relevant is Morton H. Halperin, *China and Nuclear Proliferation* (Chicago: University of Chicago Press, 1966). Still worth reading are Fred C. Ikle, "Nth Countries and Disarmament," *Bulletin of the Atomic Scientists*, Vol. 16, No. 10 (December 1960), pp. 391-394; and Fred C. Ikle, *The Violation of Arms Control Agreements: Deterrence vs. Detection* (Santa Monica, California: The Rand Corporation, RM-2609-ARPA, 1960). A thorough treatment is Mason Willrich, *Non-Proliferation Treaty: Framework for Nuclear Arms Control* (Charlottesville, Virginia: The Michie Co., 1969). Possibilities by crazy states to build up a small nuclear arsenal are clearly indicated in Ciro Zoppo, "Nuclear Technology, Weapons, and the Third World," *The Annals of the American Academy of Political and Social Science*, Vol. 386, (November 1969), pp. 113-125.

Problems of analysis and prediction of external-action capabilities are discussed in Klaus Knorr, *The War Potential of Nations* (Princeton: Princeton University Press, 1956) and in Klaus Knorr, *Military Power and Potential* (Lexington, Mass.: D.C. Heath and Co., 1970).

To move on to possibilities to control crazy states, one could start with early attempts, such as the League of Nations international conferences of repression of terrorism. To limit myself to more recent material, a series of empiric cases are discussed in Linda B. Miller, *World Order and Local Disorder: The United Nations and Internal Conflict* (Princeton: Princeton University Press, 1967). More analytical is Alan James, *The Politics of Peace-Keeping* (N.Y.: Praeger, 1969). From the United States point of view, relevant issues are examined in Lincoln P. Bloomfield and Amelia C. Leiss, *Controlling Small Wars: A Strategy for the 1970's* (N.Y.: Alfred A. Knopf, 1969); and in Alexander L. George, David K. Hall and William R. Simons, *The Limits of Coercive Diplomacy: Laos, Cuba, Vietnam* (Boston: Little, Brown, 1971). Illuminating in respect to the inadequacy of treaties as a safeguard, is Laurence W. Berlenson, *The Treaty Trap: A History of the Performance of Political Treaties by the United States and European Nations* (Washington, D.C.: Public Affairs Press, 1969).

The dependency of policy on perceptions is discussed in Konrad Kellen, *On*

Problems in Perceiving other Nations and Systems (University of California, Los Angeles: Security Studies Paper Number 15, 1968); and in Robert Jervis, "Hypotheses on Misperception," *World Politics,* Vol. 20 (1968), pp. 454-479, reprinted in James N. Rosenau, ed., *International Politics and Foreign Policy* (N.Y.: Free Press, revised ed., 1968), pp. 239-254. A relevant and rather unusual case study is Philip M. Burgess, *Elite Images and Foreign Policy Outcomes,* (Ohio: Ohio State University Press, 1967).

Relevant fallacies in United States strategic studies which hinder, inter alia, perception of the crazy state issue are discussed in Stanley Hoffman, *Gulliver's Troubles or the Setting of American Foreign Policy* (N.Y.: McGraw-Hill, 1968), especially Part Two. Additional fallacies are discussed in Fred C. Ikle, *American Shortcomings in Negotiating with Communist Powers,* Committee Print, Committee on Government Operations, U.S. Senate (Washington, D.C.: U.S. Government Printing Office, 1970), and in Nathan Leites and Charles Wolf, Jr., *Rebellion and Authority: An Analytic Essay on Insurgent Conflicts,* Chapter 2.

Bureaucratic difficulties involved in preferable policies are clearly demonstrated in Richard E. Neustadt, *Alliance Politics* (N.Y.: Columbia University Press, 1970); Morton H. Halperin, *Bureaucratic Politics and Foreign Policy* (Washington, D.C.: The Brookings Institution, forthcoming); Roger Hilsman, *The Politics of Policy Making in Defense and Foreign Affairs* (N.Y.: Harper & Row, 1971); and Alain C. Enthoven and K. Wayne Smith, *How Much is Enough?* (N.Y.: Harper & Row, 1971). Some proposals for overcoming these difficulties are presented in Yehezkel Dror, *Public Policymaking Reexamined* (San Francisco: Chandler, 1968) and Yehezkel Dror, *Design for Policy Sciences* (N.Y.: American Elsevier, 1971).

Notes

Introduction

1. There are some distinguished exceptions. See, for instance, the many relevant comments in Herman Kahn, et al., *War Termination and Concepts* (N.Y.: Hudson Institute, AD683775, June 1968), reprinted in part in Herman Kahn, "Issues of Thermonuclear War Termination," *Annals of the American Academy of Political and Social Science*, Vol. 392 (November 1970), pp. 133-172.

2. On the nature of policy sciences and its unique paradigms and orientations, see my book, *Design for Policy Sciences* (N.Y.: American Elsevier, 1971). More detailed examination of selected policy sciences concepts and applications to a number of concrete issues are included in my book, *Ventures in Policy Sciences* (N.Y.: American Elsevier, 1971).

3. Thus, I try to transform the method first applied to international relations by Morton A. Kaplan into a policy analysis methodology. See Morton A. Kaplan, *Systems and Process in International Politics* (N.Y.: John Wiley, 1957) and Morton A. Kaplan, "The Systems Approach to International Politics," in Morton A. Kaplan, ed., *New Approaches to International Relations* (N.Y.: St. Martin's Press, 1968), pp. 381-404.

Chapter 1
Common Fallacies in American Strategic Studies

1. Robert Frank Futrell, *The United States Air Force in Korea 1950-1953* (N.Y.: Duell, Sloan and Pearce, 1961), p. XVII.

2. See Nathan Leites, *The Operational Code of the Soviet Politburo* (New York: McGraw-Hill, 1951) and Alexander George, "The Operational Code: A Neglected Approach to the Study of Political Leaders and Decisionmaking," *International Studies Quarterly*, Vol. 13, No. 2 (June 1969), pp. 190-211.

3. For a fascinating and broad attempt to deal with widespread weaknesses in United States thinking on foreign policy, see Stanley Hoffmann, *Gulliver's Troubles or the Setting of Foreign Policy* (New York: McGraw-Hill, 1968), esp. Part Two.

4. See David Hackett Fischer, *Historian's Fallacies: Toward a Logic of Historical Thought*, (New York: Harper & Row, 1970).

5. See Richard E. Neustadt, *Alliance Politics* (N.Y.: Columbia University Press, 1970), Graham T. Allison, "Conceptual Models and the Cuban Missile

Crisis," *The American Political Sciences Review*, (September 1969), pp. 689-718; Morton H. Halperin, *Bureaucratic Politics and Foreign Policy*, (Washington, D.C.: The Brookings Institution, forthcoming); and Roger Hilsman, *Politics of Policy Making in Defense and Foreign Affairs* (N.Y.: Harper & Row, 1971).

6. See James N. Rosenau, ed., *Linkage Politics: Essays on the Convergence of National and International Systems* (New York: The Free Press, 1969).

7. See Fred C. Ikle, *Every War Must End* (N.Y.: Columbia University Press, 1971).

8. See Anthony Downs, *An Economic Theory of Democracy* (N.Y.: Harper, 1957) and James M. Buchanan and Gordon Tullock, *The Calculus of Consent* (Ann Arbor: The University of Michigan Press, 1962).

9. For a very readable exposition of this concept and some of its problems and implications, see Richard Zeckhauser and Elmer Shaefer, "Public Policy and Normative Economic Theory," in Raymond A. Bauer and Kenneth J. Gergen, ed., *The Study of Policy Formation* (N.Y.: The Free Press, 1968), pp. 27-101, esp. pp. 43-64.

10. For clarification of many related concepts, see Howard Raiffa, *Decision Analysis: Introductory Lectures on Choices Under Certainty* (Reading, Mass.: Addison-Wesley, 1968). For empirical studies on actual attitudes to risk, see Maynard W. Shelly II and Glenn L. Bryan, ed., *Human Judgment and Optimality* (N.Y.: John Wiley, 1964).

11. See Yehezkel Dror, *Design for Policy Sciences*, Chapter 10.

12. See Laurence W. Beilenson, *The Treaty Trap: A History of the Performance of Political Treaties by the United States and European Nations* (Washington, D.C.: Public Affairs Press, 1969).

13. See Fred C. Ikle, *American Shortcomings in Negotiating with Communist Powers*, Committee Print, Committee on Government Operations, U.S. Senate (Washington, D.C.: U.S. Government Printing Office, 1970).

14. For instance, see the striking discussion of fallacies in respect to insurgency in Nathan Leites and Charles Wolf, Jr., *Rebellion and Authority: An Analytic Essay on Insurgent Conflicts* (Chicago: Markham Publishing Co., 1970), Chapter 2.

Chapter 3
Probability of Crazy States

1. On the methodology of scenarios, see H.A. DeWeerd, *Political-Military Scenarios* (Santa Monica, California: The Rand Corporation, P-3535, February 1967) and Herman Kahn and Anthony J. Wiener, *The Year 2000: A Framework for Speculation on the Next Thirty-Three Years* (N.Y.: Macmillan, 1967), pp. 262-264.

2. For a series of such scenarios and an explanation of their possible—though low—probability, see Rachel Elboim-Dror and Yehezkel Dror, *The Downfall of the United States: Some Possible Scenarios* (in preparation).

Chapter 4
External-Action Capabilities of
Crazy States

1. Its best treatment is Klaus Knorr, *Military Power and Potential* (Lexington, Massachusetts: Lexington Books, D.C. Heath, 1970).

2. For this excellent concept, see Albert Wohlstetter, "Illusions of Distance," *Foreign Affairs* (January 1968), pp. 242-255.

3. On nonviolent defense systems, see, for instance, Gene Sharp, *Exploring Nonviolent Alternatives* (Boston, Mass.: Porter Sargent, 1970); and Adam Roberts, ed., *Civilian Resistance as a National Defense: Non-Violent Action Against Aggression* (Middlesex, England: Pelican Books, 1969). On mass participation in shelter building, see Frederick C. Rockett, *Management Requirements for Crisis Civil Defense Programs* (Hudson-on-Croton, N.Y.: Hudson Institute, HI-612-RR, September 1, 1966).

4. See, for instance, Albert Speer, *Inside the Third Reich: Memoirs of Albert Speer* (N.Y.: Macmillan, 1970).

5. The problem of country classification is succinctly discussed in Charles L. Taylor, "Statistical Typology of Microstates and Territories," in United Nations Institute for Training and Research, *Status and Problems of Very Small States and Territories* (N.Y.: UNITAR, Research Series No. 3, 1969), pp. 206-230.

6. See Lewis A. Frank, *The Arms Trade in International Relations* (N.Y.: Praeger, 1969).

7. For a concise discussion of the possibility of underdeveloped countries developing nuclear weapons, see Ciro Zoppo, "Nuclear Technology, Weapons, and the Third World," *The Journal of the American Academy of Political and Social Sciences*, Vol. 386, November 1969, pp. 113-125.

8. The best treatise is Mason Willrich, *Non-Proliferation Treaty: Framework for Nuclear Arms Control* (Virginia: The Michie Co., 1969).

9. For a science fiction treatment of this possibility with serious undertones, see Mordecai Roshwald, *A Small Armageddon* (London: William Heinemann, 1962).

10. See Nathan Leites and Charles Wolf, Jr., *Rebellion and Authority*, 1970.

11. For predictions of various possible ultraconventional weapons, see Nigel Calder, *Unless Peace Comes* (N.Y.: Viking Press, 1968).

12. For an important discussion of the difficulties faced by small states, see

David Vital, *The Inequality of States: A Study of the Small Power in International Relations* (Oxford: Clarendon Press, 1967).

Chapter 5
Some Preferable Strategies for
Crazy States

1. See Albert Wohlstetter, "Theory and Opposed-Systems Design," in Morton A. Kaplan, ed., *New Approaches to International Relations* (N.Y.: St. Martin's Press, 1968), pp. 19-53.
2. See Thomas C. Schelling, *Arms and Influence* (New Haven: Yale University Press, 1966), esp. pp. 36-43; and Stephen Maxwell, *Rationality in Deterrence* (London: Institute for Strategic Studies, Adelphi Paper No. 50, August 1968).
3. The best treatment is Barton Whaley, *Strategem: Deception and Surprise in War* (Cambridge, Mass.: Center for International Studies, M.I.T., C-69-9, April 1969. Abridged edition by Praeger).
4. The best treatment is still Daniel Ellsberg, *The Theory and Practice of Blackmail* (Santa Monica, California: The Rand Corporation, P-3883, July 1968), based on a series of lectures delivered in 1959.

Chapter 6
Some Preferable Countercraziness Strategies

1. An excellent discussion of frames of appreciation and the need to change them in order to improve policy-making is included in Sir Geoffrey Vickers, *The Art of Judgment: A Study of Policy Making* (London: Chapman & Hall, 1965).
2. Still unique is Roberta Wohlstetter, *Pearl Harbor: Warning and Decision* (Stanford: Stanford University Press, 1963).
3. The arguments presented in the writing of Guglielmo Ferrero are relevant. See, for instance, *The Principles of Power* (N.Y.: G.P. Putnam's Sons, 1942).
4. For a suggestion to establish Assassination Commandos, see Edward Hyams, *Killing No Murder: A Study of Assassination as a Political Means* (Bristol: Nelson, 1969), pp. 229-230. Depending on one's point of view, his suggestion can be regarded as crazy or countercrazy, but surely it is counterstylistic.
5. Thomas C. Schelling, *The Strategy of Conflict* (Cambridge, Mass.: Harvard University Press, 1960).

6. See John H. Herz, *International Politics in the Atomic Age* (N.Y.: Columbia University Press, 1969), where the important concept of impermeability is developed (especially in Chapters 2 and 3).

Chapter 7
Expected Countercraziness Behavior

1. On possible advantages of zero policy-making, see Yehezkel Dror, *Public Policymaking Reexamined* (San Francisco: Chandler, 1968), p. 136. These advantages do not exist in respect to novel and dangerous policy issues such as crazy states.

2. Weaknesses of organizational decision processes are so important a factor in hindering adoption of preferable countercraziness strategies that they deserve intense attention by interested readers. Good summaries are provided in Donald W. Taylor, "Decision Making and Problem Solving," in James March, ed., *Handbook of Organizations* (Chicago: Rand McNally, 1965), pp. 48-86; and Julian Feldman and Herschel E. Kanter, "Organizational Decision Making," ibid., pp. 614-649. See also Yehezkel Dror, *Public Policymaking Reexamined*, pp. 81-83.

About the Author

Yehezkel Dror is Head of the Public Administration Division in the Department of Political Science at the Hebrew University of Jerusalem and Director of Policy Analysis at the World Institute, Jerusalem. He studied at the Hebrew University of Jerusalem and Harvard University; was a Fellow at the Center for Advanced Study in the Behavioral Sciences in Palo Alto, California, received the Rosolio Award for significant contributions to the study and practice of public administration in Israel, and spent the years of 1968-1970 at The Rand Corporation, Santa Monica, California. Professor Dror has served as a consultant to various agencies of the Israeli Government and has extensive experience as a consultant and lecturer in other countries. His main books include *Public Policymaking Reexamined* (San Francisco: Chandler, 1968), *Design for Policy Sciences* (N.Y: American Elsevier, 1971) and *Ventures in Policy Sciences* (N.Y: American Elsevier, 1971).

Index

ABM, opposition to, 18
Absolute blackmail, 68
Actions, interpreting, 14
Adversaries:
  behavior, 6, 8
  conversion of, 64
  counterstylistic behavior, 8
  fixed, 9
  isolation of, 63
  occupation of, 69
  personification, 9
  political control of, 50
  understanding, 1
Aggression:
  religious, 23
  United States, 14
Aggressiveness, internal/external, 15
Agreements, international, keeping, 20
Air strikes, preemptive counterforce, 50
Alertness, 87–91
Alliances, manipulation of, 65–66
Armed forces:
  build-up of, 12
  external action capability, 43
Assumptions, 1

Bargaining, 86
Behavior:
  calculated and "cool," 18
  countercraziness, 93–96
  counterstylistic, 8
  expected/optimal, 6
  goal contents and, 24
  overreactive, 66
  reality and, 26
  taboo, considering, 7
  undesirable, 6
Biochemical warfare, 48, 49, 54–58
Biological weapons, 54
Blackmail, 54, 67–69
  with nuclear weapons, 68
Black market buying, 47
Border adjustment, erosion by, 65
Bureaucracy, military aid and, 13

Capitulation, 87–91
Catholic Church, noncountry entity, 28
Chemical weapons, 49
China, rapprochement with, 34
Circumstances, geopolitical analysis, 41

Communication instruments, importance, 46
Communism, potential dangers in, 34
Conflict, stylized pattern, 7–8
Conservatism, in policy-making, 54
Conventional military external-action
  instruments, 48, 49–50
Conversion, 64
"Coolness," 17–18
Counterbalancing strategy, 79–80
Countercraziness, multifactors for, 82–83
Countercraziness behavior, 93–96
Countercraziness strategies, 73–91
  readiness of, 87
Counterforce air strikes, 50
Counterpopulation strike, 52
Countries:
  classification of, 45, 46, 54
  defined, 28
  "goodness" concept for, 12–14
  infrastructure, classification by, 54
  less-than-major, weakness, 41
  wants of, identifying, 14
Craziness:
  discouraging, 78–79
  trend to, reversing, 78
Crazy states:
  characteristics, defined, 73
  concepts of, 23–30
    classification, 24
  counterbalancing, 79–80
  damage by, limiting, 85–86
  defined, 23
  detecting emergence of, 76
  deterring, 80–82
  deviation from, 26
  dimensions of, 28
  discouraging, 73–74, 77–78
  emergence of, 38, 76
  external-action capabilities, 41–58
    developing, 45
  external actions by, 60
  hindering, 77–78
  history-making impact, 31
  impact, 31, 97
  issue of, significance, 97–101
  master list of, constructing, 58
  noninstrumental, 44
    defined, 45
  occurrence of, probability, 97

115

occupation of, 84–85
optimal strategies, 60
preferable strategies, 59–72
prevention of, 74
probability of, 31–39
problem of, neglect, 3
prototypes of, 44
strategic problem, 39
variables influencing, 32
Credibility, defined, 80–81
Crisis, 8
taking advantage in, 33
Cultures:
alien, utilization of, 3
United States, exposure to, 15

Damage, limiting, 85–86
Deception, 63
Defense alliance, erosion by, 65
Delivery capability, 51
Deprivation, feelings of, 38
Desires, for U.S. standards, 14
Destruction, 69–70
Deterrence, defined, 80–82
Development, economic, 15–16
Developing countries, "goodness"/concept
for, 12–14
Developmental capabilities, 47
Diplomats, kidnapping of, 54
Disillusionment, contemporary values, 38
Domestic policy, 9–11
Domestic politics, 12
ignorance of, 11
Doomsday machine, 49
blackmail and, 68
radioactive, 53

Economic development, 15–16
Economic instruments, 47
Economics, military aid and, 13
Ends, means and, 18
Entities, 1
Erosion, 65
Escalation policies, 18
Expected behavior, 6
Expected impact significance, 97
External action capabilities, 41–58
basic features, 42
built-up of, 47
classification of, 46
concept of, 41
crazy states and, 60
defined, 41
destroying, 84
developing, 45

development of, reducing, 74–75
dimensions of, 42
estimation of, 46
infrastructure, 44
proportional size, 43
systemic absorption of, 48
transformability, 43

Fallacies, overlapping of, 4
First-strike capability, 51
Fission bombs, 51
Foreign aid, 9
Frustration, 38
Future:
present and, 5
viewing of, 5–7

Geopolitical analysis, 41
Geopolitics, concepts of, 41
Goal commitment, defined, 25
Goal contents, defined, 24
Goodness, U.S. concepts of, 12–14

High-intensity weapons, 54
History:
misreading of, 7
study of, repudiates fallacies, 5
Humanistic values, 16

Ideology:
conversion to, 64
handling of, 15
Ignorance, policies, 12
Internal multiactors, 3
Impact significance, expected, 97
Indirect blackmail, 67
Infiltration, 63
Information, access to, controlling, 75
Infraconventional military external-action
instruments, 48, 53–54
Infrastructure, 44
classification by, 54
Injustice, feelings of, 38
Insurgence, 48, 50–53
Interaction, among factors, 42
Interaction system, external actions within,
60
Internal politics, 12
International relations, concepts of,
overcoming, 87
"coolness" in, 17
International system contemporary, 94–95
Isolation, 65

Kidnapping, 54

Kissinger, Henry, 12

Learning, inhibiting, 1
Limited market buying, 48

Major countries, defined, 45
Mass media, control by, 38
Materialism, 24
Means, ends and, 19
Means-goal relations, defined, 25–26
Medium countries, defined, 45
Megapolicies, United States, 17
Microcountries:
  defined, 45
  number of, 46
Military aid, bureaucratic and economic
    purposes, 13
Military aims, strategic analysis and, 11
Military concept, image of, 5
Military external-action instruments:
  conventional, 48, 49–50
  infraconventional, 48, 53–54
  nuclear, 48, 50–53
  ultraconventional, 48, 54–58
Mind control, 38
Minor countries, defined, 45
Monopoly, erosion by, 65
Moral codes, influence of, 6
Multiactors, for countercraziness, 82–83

National Security Council, 12
Nazi ideology, 15
Negotiables, among countries, 19–20
Nixon Doctrine, 13
Noncountries:
  defined, 28
  interaction by, 42
  multiactions, 30
Non-Proliferation Treaty, 51
Nonscientific activities, tacit theories, 1
Nuclear barriers, 49
Nuclear bombs, development, 51
Nuclear capability, development, 52
Nuclear instruments, blackmail by, 68
Nuclear military external-action instru-
    ments, 48, 50–53
Nuclear proliferation, 14
Nuclear reactors, peaceful purposes di-
    verted, 51
Nuclear tactical weapons, 49
Nuclear war, limited, possibility of, 18
Nuclear weapons, fallacy of, 13

Occupation, 69
  of crazy states, 84–85

Open trade relations, 47
Optimal behavior, 6
Overlapping, of preferred strategies, 61
Overreactive behavior, 66

Paraphysical weapons, 49
Pareto Optimality, 15
Pax Americana-Sovietica, 90
Peace studies, 5
Penetration, of adversary, 50
Perceptions, 1
Poison gas, 54
Policy, strategic/domestic, 9–11
Policy analysis, justifying, 31
Policy-making:
  conservatism in, 54
  strategic, barriers to, 93
Policy science, development of, 2
Political analysis, decisions, improving, 32
Political constraints, domestic, 94
Political control, of adversary, 50
Political goals, strategic analysis and, 11–18
Political processes, domestic, erosion by 65
Politics:
  domestic, ignorance of, 12
  internal, dependency on, 12
Positive functions, fulfilling, 1
Power, responsibility and, 16
Predictions, monitoring of, 3
Preferable, concept of, 59
Preferred strategies, 59–72
  clarifying, 61
  components, 61
  defined, 59
  idealized concept, 61
  overlapping within, 61
  substrategies, 70
Prototypes, general treatment, 42
Provocation, 66–67
Present:
  future and, 5
  understanding of, fallacy, 4–5
Punishment, deterrence through, 81

Radical change, 38
Radioactive poisoning, 49
Radioactive weapons, 48, 54–58
Reactions, spasm, 18
Readiness, 87–90
Reality:
  behavioral study, 26
  concepts of, 1
  range of, 28
Redundancy, in strategic studies, 3
Religious movements, aggression in, 23

Repression, feelings of, 38
Responsibility, power and, 16
Revolt, stimulating, 84
Risk, minimizing, 17
Risk propensity, defined, 25

Sabotage, 48, 49, 50–53
Salami tactics, 65
Scenario:
  defined, 32
  Soviet Union, 34
  United States, 33–34
Science, tacit theories, 1
Second strike capability, 51, 52
Social change, radicalized, 38
Soviet Union:
  aggression, 6
  nuclear provocation by, 18
  Pax Americanus-Sovietica, 90
  scenario, 34
  supercountry, 98, 99
Spasm reactions, 18
Stalling, for time, 86
Strategic planning, 1
Strategic policy, domestic policy and, 9–11
Strategic studies:
  fallacies in, 1–21
    overcoming, 2
  redundancy in, 3
  tacit theories and, 1, 2
  U.S. fallacies in, 3
Strategies, countercraziness, 73–91
Strike capabilities, 51, 52
Style, defined, 26–30
Subcountry entities, 28
Substrategies, 73–91
  reinforced, 82
Subversion, 48, 50–53
Suggestive devices, 38
Supercountries:
  defined, 45
  significance of, 98
System, 1
  personification of, 9

Taboo behavior, 7
Tacit theories, 1, 2
  revising, 3

underlying, strength of, 16
Take-over, from within, 63
Technical innovations, use subverted, 51
Time, bargaining for, 86
Total simulation groups, 3
Total war possibilities, 18
Total occupation, 69
Trade agreement, erosion by, 65
Transformational variables, 42

Ultraconventional military external-action
    instruments, 48, 54–58
Understanding, 1
  of the present, fallacy, 4–5
Unitary entity, 9
United Arab Republic, aggression, 6
United States:
  aggressive behavior, 14
  a crazy state, 33–34
  culture, exposure to, 15
  free world concept, 34
  interests, spreading of, 12–14
  megapolicies, 17
  military doctrines, 12
  Pax Americana-Sovietica, 90
  standards of, desires for, 14
  strategic studies, fallacies in, 3
  supercountry, 98, 99
  supercraziness in, 24

Values, contemporary, disillusionment with,
    38
Variables:
  relevant, changing, 38
  transformational, 42
Vulnerability, 48

Wants, for U.S. standards, 14
War:
  nuclear, possibilities, 18
  planning of, 11
  preparation for, 5
Warsaw Pact, 34
Weakness, less-than-major countries, 41
Weapons:
  overlap among, 49
  U.S. policy, 12
World opinion, 20–21